BE A DISRUPTOR

STREETWISE LESSONS FOR ENTREPRENEURS—FROM THE MOB TO MANDATES

STRATIS MORFOGEN

Skyhorse Publishing

Skyhorse Publishing books may be purchased in bulk at special discounts for sales promotion, corporate gifts, fund-raising, or educational purposes. Special editions can also be created to specifications. For details, contact the Special Sales Department, Skyhorse Publishing, 307 West 36th Street, 11th Floor, New York, NY 10018 or info@skyhorsepublishing.com.

Skyhorse® and Skyhorse Publishing® are registered trademarks of Skyhorse Publishing, Inc.®, a Delaware corporation.

Visit our website at www.skyhorsepublishing.com.

10 9 8 7 6 5 4 3 2 1

Library of Congress Cataloging-in-Publication Data is available on file.

ISBN: 978-1-5107-7376-9
eBook ISBN: 978-1-5107-7380-6

Cover design by Brian Peterson

Printed in the United States of America

To my late parents, John and Beatrice Morfogen;
to my beautiful family: my wife, Filipa, and my daughters, Natalie,
*   Beatriz, and Isabel;*
and to author George P. Morfogen for paving the way for me.

Some names have been changed to protect the guilty.

Contents

Introduction

This is a book about a different kind of person.

It's a person who acts fearlessly, even when the fear they feel is very great. It's a person who reframes a situation when the odds are against them and who turns the odds back to their advantage. And, most important, it's about a person who runs *toward* a burning building when all the other people are running away.

Throughout time, there have been different terms for these kinds of people. The ones who think differently. Who take action when others around them are paralyzed. Who get things done.

The term for these people today—and it's not a bad one—is *disruptor*.

Disruptors can appear in any industry or field. There are disruptors in medicine, in war, in art, and so on. This book is about being a disruptor in business, something I have lived and breathed my entire life.

There are two things you should know about me before reading this book . . .

One: From the time I was four years old, I knew I'd go into the food business. It's in my blood going back three generations. When you read my story, if you're the kind of person who believes in destiny, it will seem like I had no choice. If you're a staunch advocate for free will, you'll see my journey as a series of choices—some of which I made in rebellion to that destiny itself. The truth is, it's a bit of both.

Two: I never thought this journey would reveal that made men can be more honorable than MBAs, and that out of betrayal and ruin can come amazing, undreamed-of opportunity. And while I'm at it, I never, *ever* thought I'd end up a specialist in Asian cuisine. (That part isn't my blood or birthright—but it has become an essential ingredient to the journey I've taken from a little kid washing dishes at the family chophouse to today, watching people eat some damn good dumplings.)

More than simply being my personal story, this book lays out the lessons from my life that I believe can be useful resources for the next generation of disruptors rising today.

My goal in writing this is to make clear how disruptors impact the business world each and every day, and how entrepreneurs can learn from them—and eventually become disruptors themselves.

As I said, this book is about a different kind of person. I am that kind of person, and I hope, after reading this, that you decide to become that kind of person, too.

CHAPTER ONE:

Think the Unthinkable

From my earliest days in the restaurant business, I had experiences that laid the groundwork for my understanding of what it takes to be a disruptor. I saw, firsthand, what the advantages are of thinking differently and tackling problems from a new perspective. But I also understood that an effective disruptor has to gain a full understanding of the world they intend to disrupt. Just like an experimental jazz musician can break all the musical rules to create something new and wonderful, but first they need to learn all the basics of their instrument. The importance of knowing the basics and becoming the kind of young person upon whom nothing was lost was made extremely clear to me early on. I also saw that the restaurant world—and the business world, more broadly—is one in which people often say one thing and do another. Moreover, it's a world in which people act as though certain laws are immutable when there is actually quite a bit of wiggle room. As I show in this chapter, a disruptor realizes that laws and rules are things made by men and women—and men and women can challenge them!

Are disruptors born or made?

This is what everybody wants to know. It's also the wrong question. Whether a disruptor is born or made doesn't matter. What matters is that a disruptor is different. A disruptor is anyone who is going to come at problems and opportunities in an entirely new way and who is going to use new ideas and new technologies to remake them.

When I look back on the story of my own life—as someone who has challenged convention and come up with innovations that have brought profound change to my industry—it feels like I could not have been any other kind of person.

Part of this is doubtless something in my DNA, but part comes from the remarkable upbringing I was lucky enough to have.

However you get there—it doesn't matter if it's nature or nurture—you have to be different. Disruptors are *very* different. They think differently, act differently, and their skill sets often don't fit with convention. And that's precisely where their power comes from. That's what allows them to win.

* * *

I was born into the restaurant business. The story starts with my grandfather Nick, who immigrated to the United States back in the 1890s. My granduncle Paul had partnered with a man named Chris Pappas, as well as his brothers Sam and Jimmy. My grandfather Nick joined them in 1910.

Times were hard in the old days, and it was a very different world. Grandpa Nick had to change his last name from Morfogenis to

Morfogen just to get a lease. Nobody would rent him space for his restaurant if he had an exotic, Mediterranean-sounding name. But with one that *might* be Anglo-Saxon . . . there was a chance it could happen.

Despite the prejudices of the day, Nick and the rest of the family grew the restaurant, Pappas, into a success. Politicians, celebrities, and industrialists came to eat there. Through their blood, sweat, and hard work, Pappas remained successful and profitable. It was one of *the* places to see and be seen in New York City until about 1960.

The Morfogens were quick to assimilate, and also to assert that they were just as American as anyone else. My family members served food to every US president from the 1920s through the 1950s. And I'm proud to say I've personally served Clinton, Obama, Trump, and Al Gore!

John, my father, started working for my grandfather when he was just eleven years old, right at the end of the Second World War. My father had been living in Sparta, in a town called Anavrati up in the mountains. Despite its remote location, it was known as the place where more Nazis were killed than in any other part of Greece. By the tender age of eleven, my father had already seen horrible atrocities of all sorts. The occupying Nazis had a policy whereby they'd execute ten civilians for every one of their own who was killed. It was a grim existence, even for children. My father could recall hiding underneath horse and cow manure—with his five siblings and my grandmother—to save themselves from these Nazi selections.

When he got to the States, my father started off by delivering groceries and vegetables. Then he was eventually brought in to work inside the restaurant at Pappas. (One by one, his other siblings from Greece were brought over to join him in the United States. By the late forties, they had all successfully made the voyage!)

At Pappas, my father learned the ins and outs of the restaurant business through his uncle Paul. It was Paul Morfogen who was the first to really *master* how the business worked.

My father worked for about ten years with Paul at Pappas. Then, in 1956, he ventured out on his own, opening his first restaurant, the Chelsea Chop House on Eighth Avenue at 23rd Street in Manhattan. He did this with $8,000 he'd saved from working at Pappas. (That would be about $75,000 today.)

Chelsea Chop House did pretty well from the start—not gang-busters, but not too bad, either. It was moving along. Getting by. But then something important happened. A disruption. My family's first major disruption of the restaurant industry. (It would not be the last!)

Back in those days, most restaurant workers had to be unionized. Organizations like the Hotel Employees and Restaurant Employees Union (HERE) were dominant in New York and boasted thousands of members. Unsatisfied with the work he was getting from his union employees at Chelsea Chop House, my father did the unthinkable and simply fired them. At the time, he was told by his peers: "You can't do that! They're union! There'll be consequences." My father did it anyway. He replaced the union workers with members of his own family—nephews, cousins, uncles, and so forth.

> My father realized that he could disrupt the system and accept the consequences. Everyone had warned him of the dangers of de-unionizing his restaurants, but my father understood there would be benefits, as well—and he was willing to take that risk!

What followed were massive protests and union pickets outside of Chelsea Chop House. It received coverage in the *New York Times* and lots of other media outlets. Many of the papers ran with xenophobic headlines to the effect of IMMIGRANT KICKS OUT AMERICAN WORKERS.

But all of this had the opposite effect of what everyone expected!

Once people heard about the Greek-run steakhouse with the brazen immigrant owner, they wanted to try it. And when they did, they loved it! (True, some people avoided crossing a picket line, but many more decided to come in and see what all the fuss was about.)

Soon, my father was being celebrated by those who disliked unions in the hospitality industry. He had shown that things could be done in a different way if someone merely had the gumption to do it. Chelsea Chop House became a roaring success. At the same time, my dad's brothers, George and Peter, returned from serving in Korea, and they became partners in the restaurant.

The triumvirate arrangement worked well at first, but soon the three brothers started to feel constrained by working so closely together in the same place every day. The good news was that due to the success they were having, the time was right to expand.

The brothers soon opened five new locations; three were in Queens, in Howard Beach, Bellerose, and Flushing; and two were on Long Island, one in Rockville Centre and one in Lawrence. Three brothers and six restaurants was a better ratio; they didn't feel like they were always on top of one another. That arrangement more or less continued within my family until about 1980.

So where did I come in?

I was raised in this mix of entrepreneurs and disruptors—who also just happened to be my family members—and started working at the Chelsea Chop House in Howard Beach, Queens, when I was just six years old. This life was so far removed from the experience of typical six-year-olds that you may find this part of my tale hard to believe . . . but if you come from a family business, or you've worked in a family business, then I have a feeling my story will ring true!

The most important thing to understand is that my upbringing allowed me to see and experience a world that was *vastly different* from what most children are ever exposed to. It was as though, at an early age, I got to peek behind the curtain and see how the machinery of the world *really* worked.

I started working out on the floor of the restaurant with my dad doing little tasks here and there. It was 1973. There was always an interesting mix of customers and characters, but one of the first things I noticed was that my dad was always especially gracious to this one diminutive, elderly man who was a regular customer. Even at six years old, I could tell that this man was distinguished and important. My father made sure to give him the best table and the best service. I also noticed that *nobody ever addressed him by his name.* Yet I knew his name because I would always hear the managers say things like: "Make sure Mr. Gambino gets table number ten!" or "Get Mr. Gambino's drink ready!"

I knew a lot for a six-year-old, but I didn't know that Carlo Gambino was the head of the Gambino crime family and inarguably the most powerful person in any of the five mafia families of New York.

So, what did I do? (Remember, I'm six . . .)

One evening, Mr. Gambino comes in with a small group of men, and as always, he seems to be trying to stay underneath the radar. Anyone could tell he does not want to be recognized.

I walk up to the table with my water pitcher to pour everyone's water, and I say, "Good evening, Mr. Gambino."

You could have heard a pin drop. Everyone froze. I could see the alarm in the man's eyes. He's thinking, "I've taken all this trouble to keep a low profile, and a *six-year-old* knows who I am!"

But I'll never forget what happened next. The other gentlemen at the table all started laughing. Then Gambino laughed, too. He motioned that I should come closer.

"C'mere kid," he said. "Put the water down and sit next to me."

I obeyed, and Gambino put his arm around me. He reached into his pocket, took out a twenty-dollar bill, and gave it to me. Then he said: "'Hi' is enough."

I looked across the dining room and saw my father watching what was happening. His expression said: "Oh my God; Stratis is *sitting with the gangsters*! What's going on?"

I heard the men still laughing as I walked back to my father. My dad took me in the back and asked what had happened. Still bewildered, I told him: "Dad, all I did was go over the table, pour water, and say, 'Good evening, Mister Gambino.'"

My father pointed out that we all called Gambino "sir" because he didn't want his name to be mentioned. My father wasn't mad at me, though. My father understood my error had not been purposeful.

In the end, I got twenty dollars and learned some valuable lessons about discretion, and about how the

> The restaurant industry was full of unspoken protocols and procedures that I didn't understand as a kid. Why did we greet some customers by name, but *never* do that with Mr. Gambino? As time went by and I began to understand how the world really worked, it became clear to me that there was much here to disrupt and innovate . . . but also much to understand. Before attempting to disrupt something, you need to learn how it works completely!

world of adults *really* works. I also understood that the floor of a restaurant could be a world of hidden protocols and secret conventions. And if I were going to succeed, I'd need to learn all of them.

As the years passed, I learned that discretion was important in very situation, but also that it meant different things at different times. Working in a restaurant, you see men with women who are not their wives. You see powerful people who want things a certain way. You see blue-collar workers, politicians, and criminals—all interacting together at once. (Far in the future, in 2009, a hedge fund was meeting in one of my restaurants, and I glimpsed a PowerPoint. It turned out this was billionaire financier John Paulson's hedge fund, and their presentation said they were going to initiate a hostile takeover of Bank of America the next day. It's amazing what you see working in restaurants!)

Because of this, I was a fast developer when it came to what today might be called "emotional intelligence." I gained a keen understanding of how to deal with people of all different types. By the age of ten, I had street smarts that most adults don't have at thirty.

But there was a trade-off. A kid doesn't become so canny about the adult world at a young age without paying some price. And for me, the price was that once I saw that world, I didn't want any other.

You see, in addition to working in my father's restaurant, I attended school like any other kid. I had trouble feeling engaged by any of the things we studied in the classroom. (Other than math skills, which I saw could be useful in the business world, it was a challenge for me to care about the subjects the teachers taught us.) Living and working every night in the world of adults also made me feel separated from my schoolmates socially. Not only were they interested in different things, but it was also clear that their *lives* were very different in a fundamental way. They were still treated like little kids and had only the responsibilities of children. What was more, they had different plans for themselves. They anticipated futures different from mine. My schoolmates were going to follow courses charted by the world of traditional schooling and then find places for themselves within the status quo. Lawyers, doctors, teachers, accountants, firefighters—they were each going to be one of these things, and they were perfectly fine with that.

I already understood that whatever the future held for me, it would involve being independent, making my own way, and living and dying by my street smarts.

The word *disruptor* did not then exist as it does today, but let's just say I was beginning to get the general idea.

* * *

My father continued to act as a mentor to me as the years went by. I sincerely looked up to him. Whenever there was a chance for me to become a part of his world in any new way, I always took it.

It may sound like a strange milestone to celebrate, but I was never so proud as when sometime in the mid-to-late 1970s my father was asked to do a series of radio commercials for American Express. By that time, my father had become perhaps the most prominent restaurateur in New York. Amex did not traditionally select restaurateurs as their spokespeople—especially ones with ethnic accents—so this was quite an accomplishment. I can still remember my excitement at turning on the radio and hearing his voice advising listeners that they could come to Chelsea Chop House and use their American Express card to buy anything that wasn't nailed to the wall.

It was a remarkable time for my dad and for our entire family. Our fortunes were on the rise, and I felt like I was playing a small part in that.

* * *

Perhaps the most special moment of apprenticeship with my father occurred when he started taking me to the Fulton Fish Market.

First established in 1822, the Fulton Fish Market is the largest seafood market in the United States, and the second largest anywhere in the world. It's the place where practically every serious player in the New York restaurant business goes to buy their fish.

To give you a sense of how important our weekly trips to the Fulton Fish Market were, when I was ten years old, my mother announced that she had planned a surprise trip for me and my siblings—my brother, Nick, and my sister, Helen—to go with her on a four-day vacation to Disney World. Any typical American kid would have been over the moon!

But I, already, was not a typical kid.

As my siblings jumped around celebrating this news, I soberly informed my mother that if it was all right with her, I would prefer to stay in New York with my father so I wouldn't miss our trip to the Fulton Fish Market.

In a way, that market *was* my Disney World.

I loved the energy of the Fulton Fish Market. There was no place like it that I knew. It was full of action and adventure, and even danger. And unlike the things you could expect to experience at Disney World, this stuff was all *real*.

When I went to the Fulton Fish Market with my father, the adventures—and the life lessons—began the very moment he parked his truck.

My dad had an informally assigned parking space at 248 Dougherty, near the market, where he'd park up on the curb. (That number and spot was the street address, but also my father's exclusive ID.) My father paid the local racketeers for the spot. Whenever

> The Fulton Fish Market was another great example of understanding something tip to tail before you disrupt it. As a child, I gained a better understanding of the Fulton Fish Market than any other kid in the world. Years later, I would use new technology to disrupt that same market . . . but only my background knowledge and "family" connections made that disruption possible.

my father made purchases at the market, he could just give the vendor the street address where his truck was parked, and the runners—who were called fishmongers—would deliver his purchase to his truck.

I remember the first time I watched my father park his truck at his assigned spot and then give a mysterious man standing nearby forty dollars. I asked him, "Why are you giving that man money? Does he work for the city?" My father explained to me that this was simply the politics of the market. If you paid the gentleman, then nothing would get stolen from your truck while you were there, and all the deliveries to your truck would arrive just fine.

What happened if you *didn't* pay was driven home a few weeks later.

On another trip to the market, my father and I passed a man who had just finished parking his truck. When asked to pay, he started screaming at the gentleman collecting money: "Fuck you; you don't work for the city!"

The gentleman in question promptly produced an icepick and popped the tires on the man's truck. There were cops half a block away, and they took care not to notice anything that was going on. (This was New York in the seventies! You don't pay? An icepick goes in your tires.)

I was bracingly aware that these things I was seeing held important lessons—the kind of lessons I was not going to learn on weekdays between 7:00 a.m. and 3:00 p.m. (My school did occasionally have cops come to our classes to give us lectures about staying on the straight and narrow, but information about how to look away at the right time when fees were being collected was somehow always omitted from their lectures . . .)

Anyhow, after parking our truck, my father and I would work our way into the market proper. It was two football fields full of vendors selling every kind of fish you could imagine. My father was active the whole time—inspecting, haggling, chatting, picking up fish to check the quality. All of it was electrifying to me.

I learned that there were tricks the vendors could use to soak the newbies and/or buyers who simply weren't careful. For example, the most common was mixing in ice with the fish so that when it was weighed you paid for ice and not for fish. "Icing the scale" it was called.

Another trick was selling a box of fish with great-looking fish on top, but lousy fish on the bottom. My father knew this trick and would always flip the contents of the box over when the fish were put on the scale. (Pretty soon, the vendors all realized that he did this and would direct him to certain boxes of fish that were good all the way through.)

My father introduced me to all his regular vendors, and also to the heads of the market who were connected to La Cosa Nostra. The real boss of the market at the time was Alphonse "Allie Shades" Malangone, who was part of the Genovese crime family. But to me, he was just another guy keeping his hands warm beside one of the street-side garbage cans with a fire burning inside. Every time I saw him, I got a "Hey kid! How's your dad?" At the time, I had no idea of the extent of Allie's forbidding reputation; he just felt like a member of our extended family.

My uncle George—son of my granduncle Paul—would also run into us at the market. At the time, George was the buyer for the Grand Central Oyster Bar. That made him the largest buyer at the market, period. When he walked onto the scene, people just stopped whatever they were doing and watched him. He had the most money to spend, and everyone knew it. He could sometimes drop $100,000 in a single day on fish, and that's in 1970s money!

In addition to George, we would also sometimes encounter my uncle Gus. He owned a restaurant named Moby Dick. We'd all meet for a family coffee nearby and share tips on which vendors had the best product that day.

One story that sticks in my mind from this era concerns the day my father bought an eight-hundred-pound box of Alaskan halibut. My father and the vendor, Herb Slavin, were absolutely screaming at each other as they haggled over the price of the fish. Herb was saying,

"Eighty-five cents!" and my father was saying, "Eighty!" I'd never seen my father get so animated. Both men were using language and terms you wouldn't use today. It was: "You fucking Jew!" and "You fucking Greek!" (This was one of my first trips to the market with my dad, and I didn't yet know that Herb and my father went way back; this antagonism was ultimately done out of jocular love for each other. It was just another part of doing business!)

Anyhow, I was so alarmed by their arguing that I spoke up and said, "Dad, here! I've got a nickel you can have if that will make the difference!"

My father stopped haggling and sat me down on a wet box of fish. (My pants stank like fish all day!) He calmly explained to me that this matter concerned a difference of eight hundred nickels, which I certainly *did not* have.

But it all worked out in the end. Herb was so amused by my attempt to intercede that he gave my dad the price he wanted.

These sorts of exchanges were my *real* classes. They let me understand which parts of my schooling I might use in business one day, and which parts weren't going to mean much out in the real world.

I also learned that people could argue like crazy over business matters but still respect or even love each other. Luckily, even as a kid, I was wise enough to understand that this sort of fighting—and the sort of words Herb and my father threw at each other, in particular—weren't things I should ever repeat around my school friends.

* * *

Another lesson I learned from my father early on was not to give up even when the language of a contract (or even a law) seems to be against you. If you feel you're in the right, then make your case. Literally, if you have to.

In the early 1970s, my father received an eviction notice from the landlord of the Chelsea Chop House in Howard Beach. My father was taken by surprise. However, he did a little checking and found out that the landlord was in the right. My father and his brothers had made a horrible error and simply forgotten who was in charge of managing the lease. Each one of them had thought another was on top of it, so nothing had been done, and the lease had simply run out.

Compounding the disaster was the fact that my father had recently done a complete gut renovation of the restaurant. This had cost him hundreds of thousands of dollars—the equivalent to millions today.

My father could have simply given up. After all, the landlord was in the right according to the law. The lease had indeed expired. My father could have slunk away, closed his restaurant despite the recent renovation, and eaten an enormous loss.

But my father did not give up. When the landlord proved intractable, my father took him to court. My father and his legal team made the case that even though he had technically allowed the lease to expire—by accident—he had shown "good faith" by investing in the space he was renting. Because of this, it would be unreasonable for any sensible person to conclude that my father had intended not to renew the lease.

> Disruptors succeed because they fight for what's right. When they see a better way to do something, they insist that it be done. Whether you are facing an unfair law, unjust regulation, or a rule that simply makes no sense—you should challenge it, disrupt it, do whatever it takes to makes your case that things should be different. *Never* lie down and say: "Well, what can I do? Those are the rules."

The case went to court, and a judge found in favor of my father. He was allowed to renew his lease. (The court case became precedent-setting and is now even taught in law school classes. You can look it up: "J.N.A. Realty Corp. v. Chelsea.")

The American justice system decided that when it is obvious that someone meant to renew a lease, but failed to do so simply because of an oversight, they should be allowed to have the option to renew it when that oversight is revealed.

My father had disrupted the very legal system itself! Moreover, he had taught me a lesson. There are laws, but *laws can be changed.* There are contracts, but contracts can be unfair and wrong. And rulings can always be overruled.

When you're in a situation where even the law seems against you, you should keep fighting if you still think you're right. Things can go your way. My dad was living proof!

TAKEAWAYS FOR FUTURE DISRUPTORS

- **Disruptors are willing to think the unthinkable and do the undoable.**
- **You can't disrupt a system before you gain an effective understanding of that system.**
- **No contract is unbreakable. Never act like one is.**

CHAPTER TWO

The Mindset of a Disruptor—Think Different!

The life of a disruptor is a journey, not a destination. Plan to be a disruptor your whole life. Plenty of people come up with a single innovation or disruption that allows them to become successful . . . only to have that success stolen away. A disruptor must always keep their guard up and defend whatever they have built. This is a hard lesson to learn, and an even harder one to implement. But making sure you keep an eye on your enterprise is part of being a lifelong disruptor—which is the only way to be. You'll need to erase from your mind the paradigm that there is only one way to solve a problem. When you are presented with options, ask yourself: "Why is this the paradigm? Are these the only options? What if there are others?" This leads naturally into considerations of your business. When a venture is not successful, look at the broader reasons. The most likely culprit may not be the guilty one. Finally, realize that the metrics by which you are

judged may not be the ones that truly matter to you. As this chap-
ter will show, my own life had many examples of being judged by
criteria that were not meaningful to me. As a result, I was con-
stantly underestimated. It's a common occurrence for disruptors!

My dad's disruption of the industry model had succeeded, and his restaurant empire continued to expand. However, he eventually reached a point where he wanted to go out on his own entirely and no longer partner with any of his brothers. That would mean winding down the Chelsea Chop House locations. It so happened that fate would have a hand in easing that transition along. The way things went down also provided another very important life lesson for me. My father had spent his life achieving success by disrupting the dominant model—but opportunists were waiting to take advantage of his hard work and steal what my father had built for themselves. I learned early on that a disruptor must be ever watchful, and always be on the lookout for swindlers and criminals.

In the Chelsea Chop House location in Rockville Centre, my dad employed a man named Mike Berthebes as a manager. Berthebes was a distant cousin of ours somehow. Initially, my dad hadn't wanted to employ him—he just didn't get a good vibe from the guy—but our uncle Pete was close with him and had insisted on it.

My dad's intuition about Berthebes turned out to be right on the money. Unbeknownst to us, Berthebes had started stealing customer credit card numbers. He then used them to create fraudulent accounts at Clappers Clothing Store in Garden City, Long Island (some employees there were colluding with him), and engage in what today we call identity theft. Before long, the feds busted the ring and arrested Berthebes along with several of the employees at the department store. The arrests broke in the press, along with the details of how the scheme had worked. Business at Chelsea Chop House in

Rockville Centre immediately dropped by 50 percent. This was back when credit cards were still a new technology (with which some consumers were not yet completely comfortable), and nobody wanted to eat at a place where your credit card numbers were apparently unsafe.

Berthebes was put on trial and found guilty. My father wanted him to go away for a long time. But at sentencing, my uncle Peter, still his friend to the end, pled for the judge to go easy on him. Apparently, this worked. Though he was eligible to receive up to seven years behind bars, he walked away with three years' probation. But as far as we were concerned, the damage was done.

> If my father hadn't been ready to wind down the Chelsea Chop House in Rockville Centre, this scandal would have been ruinous for us. Always keep an eye out for criminals and make an example of them whenever possible!

The brand of our Chelsea Chop House restaurants was tarnished, and this location was tarnished beyond saving. (I will note that Berthebes is still working in the restaurant industry, which disturbs me deeply. He has been lauded by magazines for stunts like once-a-year events where he feeds the homeless in his restaurants. *Newsday* once featured his charitable work, and their profile of him made the man look like some kind of hero! I wish reporters would dig a little deeper and learn the whole story about the people they profile.)

The larger lesson here was that you have to take crooks seriously, and you always have to protect yourself. The damage done by a single bad employee can come back to reflect badly on your whole business. (The Rockville Centre location of Chelsea Chop House was briefly reincarnated as The Atlantis Diner—another business my family owned—but it was only in that location briefly. We still own the property, and our current tenant is The Golden Reef Diner.)

* * *

Our family had to deal with crooks again just a few years later. However, in this second instance, it was clear that my father had now learned his lesson. Let me tell you about Peter and Jimmy Salates . . .

Just like Berthebes, these two were distant relatives who'd come to us looking for work. My father and uncles had given them positions as managers at Longhorn Trails Steakhouse, a business we opened briefly that ran concurrent with the Chelsea Chop Houses.

My father was always aware that the numbers weren't adding up right at Longhorn. Business was great and people were dropping lots of money, but the profits never seemed to come in at the end of the day. The restaurant should have been making us much more money than it was.

My father suspected that Peter and Jimmy were stealing, but he couldn't yet prove it. So, what did my father do? He decided to be proactive about defending what he had built! Specifically, he started discreetly marking the cash that went into the safe at the end of each night. Then he could tell if a bill came through Longhorn because it would be discreetly tagged with a pen or pencil mark. (In addition to the lack of profits, my father was also suspicious because the head of the local bank had called him to tip him off that when Jimmy came in to drop off money, he was dividing the deposits into two accounts— and one was in his own name.)

This was a long-term play by my dad, but it paid off. After the trap had been set for a while, and he'd been marking bills for months and months, he finally made his move.

My father told Peter and Jimmy that he was looking to sell Longhorn. Suddenly, the pair said they had the money and would like to buy it. (My father knew Peter and Jimmy *never* had any money. Still, he played along.) My father agreed to a price of $300,000. Peter and Jimmy asked if my dad would accept cash at closing . . . just as he had expected they would.

My father agreed, and they set up a meeting to do the sale. Peter and Jimmy arrived with the money, and my father arrived with some of his people (including me) and said he wanted to count the cash then and there. Peter and Jimmy told him sure. But my dad wasn't just counting it; he was checking for his own markings. And what did he find? Sure enough, about $250,000 of the $300,000 was marked. They had stolen that money from the Longhorn safe and were trying to buy a steakhouse from my dad with his own money.

How did it end?

Let's just say that there was a physical altercation—I'd never seen my father grab anybody by the throat before!—and Jimmy ended up "falling down some stairs."

My father walked away with his stolen money, and I took another dose of an old life lesson: you must always protect what you have built! Those who betray you can be family members. In fact, those who betray you may be *likely* to be family members. You can't let your guard down just because someone is your distant cousin!

> My father's treatment of Peter and Jimmy was harsh, but it was what they deserved. What's more, it got the word on the street. Now everyone knew my father was the kind of guy who would defend his interests and never allow himself to be robbed.

* * *

The years 1978 and 1979 were a time of transition for my father. The Chelsea Chop House name remained tarnished from the Berthebes scandal, and it was tough to get new projects off the ground.

An important lesson in the restaurant industry is that management and ownership are conflated in the mind of the consumer. That is to say: they're the same thing as far as customers go. The fact that it was a manager at Chelsea Chop House who'd been crooked and now that manager was fired didn't matter to the customers. Unfairly or not, customers don't care how a problem came about, or if it has been remedied. When they have a bad association with a business, they don't probe any deeper into the details.

After splitting with his brothers, my father found a great location to open a new restaurant in Syosset, Long Island. The property was seven thousand square feet. There were three little stores with space for small businesses (such as a nail salon) and one larger space for a restaurant. There was actually already a restaurant in the space called Manero's. The way my father approached obtaining this space ended up being a powerful lesson in disruption for me.

My father began by meeting with Tony Dowd, the founder and owner of Manero's. My father told him, "I want to open a restaurant here. I love your space! Would you consider closing Manero's? Can we make a deal?"

Dowd replied that he wanted $400,000 for a three-year lease, but the option had to be agreed to by

> My father could have accepted Dowd's offer: "Either take the lease from me at the price I name or pass on the opportunity entirely." But my father disrupted that model and found another way forward: he bought the entire building!

the landlord. It was gradually revealed that Dowd himself was just a tenant; he didn't own the space and would be subleasing to us. My father considered this carefully. (Although just twelve years old at the time, I was present at these meetings and carefully watching the chess game between my father and Dowd.)

My father was not satisfied with the terms Dowd kept coming back with, so he took a different approach (also providing a lesson for me): He kept digging. He kept peeling the onion. He looked at new ways to solve the problem.

Again (though we didn't have the term then), he was being a disruptor.

My father did some research on his own and found that the owner of the property was an elderly woman named Mrs. Showbitz who lived in Palm Beach, Florida.

My father got on a plane to Palm Beach, knocked on her door, and said he wanted to buy the property. She was open to the idea and said that for $450,000 my father could buy the property outright—the restaurant space and the three retail spaces. My father, canny as he was, said he was thinking more along the lines of $350,000. Eventually, they compromised at $400,000.

My father bought the whole property for what Dowd wanted for a three-year lease of just the restaurant space.

I'll never forget going with my father to eat at Manero's after the sale went through. Dowd came over and sat down with us. He got all chatty and eventually worked things around to business, asking my father if he was still interested in making a deal. My father said, "Don't worry about that. You'll get a notice in about six months to leave your restaurant when the lease is up."

Dowd said, "What the fuck are you talking about?"

My father said, "I'm your new landlord, and I'm not renewing your lease."

I'll never forget the stunned look on Dowd's face. He'd been trying to put one over on my father, and my father had put one over on him! How? Through diligence, creativity, and by not accepting that there was just one way to solve a problem.

After Manero's closed down, my father opened a successful restaurant in that space called King of the Sea.

My father and his family became pretty wealthy because they always owned the properties where their restaurants were located. So, if the businesses didn't do too well, they could still sell the business and the land underneath it. In the restaurant industry, we call this "key money." What made my father's generation wealthy was that they believed in owning the property whenever possible. (It's also colloquially known as "the immigrant's pension," though my father never loved that term. I also used to call it "the uneducated's pension.")

And what of Dowd? He actually moved across the street and reopened Manero's in a building that was right next to a Crazy Eddie's appliance store, but it was never the same.

* * *

An interesting tradition my father had that I should note: He always gave me a dollar on my birthday for however many years old I was. He'd give me one dollar when I turned one, a couple of bucks when I turned two, and so forth. When I was old enough, I told him, "I can't wait until I'm fifty!"

Now, this wasn't the only money I had at the time. Between the ages of six and ten, I could make between one and five dollars a night working in my dad's restaurant.

My father would always make a point to pay me at the end of every evening. (Whenever it seemed like times were tough, I'd always tell my dad, "Keep it! You need it more than I do.") Often, my father would give me my pay when there were still guests in the restaurant and make a point to do it in front of them. It was a little gimmick that the diners always thought was cute, giving a buck or two to a little kid.

Anyhow, here's the important thing: *I always knew the value of a dollar.* My father made sure that this was as essential as eating and breathing for me. Knowing what things cost and knowing the value of my own labor has always been a part of my life. My father made damn sure of that.

> It's important to know the value of a dollar, but it's also important to be kind to those you work with.

24

During this time, my father also taught me the value of kindness, and having the backs of your employees.

My father had a dishwasher in the Chelsea Chop House location in Howard Beach named Paul. He came over as an immigrant and worked as a dishwasher. One night there was an ICE raid. Paul didn't have papers. Quickly, my father took all the soiled napkins and the rags used to clean the fryers and grills and threw them on top of Paul while he hid in a laundry bag. It couldn't have been nice for Paul, but it worked. ICE never found him. Paul always said that if my father hadn't done that, he would have been sent back to Greece. (Twenty years later, Paul bought that location of Chelsea Chop House and ran it until 1987 as the Chelsea House.)

* * *

When my father sold the last Chelsea Chop House in 1979, that left just one restaurant that my dad still partially owned along with his brothers: the Atlantis Diner. The Atlantis was a Greek diner and was not the most remarkable place in terms of my family's restaurant holdings. However, the Atlantis turned out to have other important lessons to teach me.

At the age of twelve, I was working there as a busboy. One of the most important things my dad taught me during this period was to work for what I wanted so that I'd learn the value of a dollar. It's something I try to impart to my own kids today.

I'll never forget being twelve and asking my dad if he'd buy me a new stereo system. How did he respond? He took out the schedule for the diner and added one more day a week for me to work as a dishwasher. That was his answer.

"You want it? Sure, you can have it. If you work for it."

When I finally got the stereo, this taught me the value of it. It also taught me to take care of it. No matter who you are or what you want, when you get it, you'll treat it better if you bought it yourself. Because of my father, I knew this at a young age.

I made the rounds as a busboy, often working in different properties owned by my family. Among the best assignments was working under my uncle Peter as a busboy at the Chelsea Chop House in Flushing.

There, I became a die-hard Mets fan and found myself serving such greats as Tommie Agee, Cleon Jones, Ed Kranepool (with whom I remain friends today), and Yogi Berra.

Yogi and I also became friends. Later in my career, when I became financially successful, I was able to surprise my dad with a couple of private dinners with Yogi. Hearing Yogi and my dad—who was a Brooklyn Dodgers fanatic—talk about the Yankees/Dodgers rivalry was priceless. (Later, Yogi gave us a tour of his personal museum at Montclair State University in New Jersey!)

My time at the Atlantis was also valuable because it let me see all the challenges that come with trying to do something new and innovative. (I had to learn to expect these challenges when I finally went out on my own.)

With Atlantis, my father was looking to raise the bar of what a Greek diner could provide. The goal of Atlantis was to bring higher-quality food into a Greek diner setting. There would be fresh fish, not frozen fish, for example. This translated into a better quality of food being served.

Great, right?

It *was* great, but, as my father quickly learned, it was not always what his customers were expecting.

Even when they're being surprised by something nice, customers can still sometimes react badly to surprises. I'll never forget the night a lady came in and ordered halibut. When she was brought her food, she made a big scene.

"*This* isn't halibut!" she cried. "You're serving me the wrong fish!"

What my father knew was that this woman was accustomed to ordering halibut and being served cheap, frozen cod, which was often substituted for halibut by second-rate restaurants. (These places also liked to substitute mako shark for swordfish.)

In most cases, my father was understanding when a customer seemed confused at tasting actual fresh halibut for the first time. But this woman wasn't expressing confusion. Rather, she was attacking my father, in his own place of business, in front of other customers. Moreover, she was speaking falsehoods. The food on her plate *was* halibut. Good quality, too!

> You can offer your customer a product that you know is superior, but it won't work out if *they* don't know it's superior!

So, what did my father do? He went back into the kitchen and picked up a whole fresh halibut. It was about five feet long and sixty pounds. He brought it out and smacked it down on the table in front of the lady. Several other guests literally jumped out of their seats when my father brought down the fish.

"*This* is a halibut!" my father said. "This is what I serve in this diner. If you're looking for something else, you can walk a mile down the road to another diner, and they'll serve you the cheap, fake halibut you're used to. But don't ever come in here and question my honesty again!"

(I can only imagine what my father would have been like if he were still around today, in the age of Yelpers, answering spurious online attacks about his food!)

It was a surprising interaction to be sure, but as I aged, I came to understand why this was in fact a teachable moment. When you're trying something new, or disrupting the status quo, you're going to be attacked and questioned. People may express that they don't like your new product or your new way of doing things—that's one thing. But if they assert things about your business that are false, you can't let it slide. Whether the error is big or small, you have to correct them. People may not like the way you do things, but they still have to tell the truth about it.

> **Just as you defend your enterprise from thieves, so too must you defend it from spurious accusations!**

Sadly, the end of the Atlantis story is that, in this case, my father truly was ahead of his time.

After it had struggled for a while, my father sold the place to traditional diner operators who changed the name to Golden Reef, rebranded, and brought back all the frozen, fake fish people were used to. (The real estate had only cost my dad $300,000 ten years before, but these operators paid my dad $1 million for a twenty-five-year lease, so my dad still made money. Again, the immigrant's pension. Sometimes the business is worth more dead when you own the property.)

People just weren't ready for the real thing.

* * *

Another lesson I learned from my father was that location matters. This is a valuable lesson for anybody who is thinking about opening up a business.

I grew up in Queens. And even as a kid, I was very entrepreneurial. There were always extra fruits and vegetables around our house that my dad would bring home from the restaurants. So, what did I do? I set up a fruit and vegetable stand along the boulevard near our home, and pretty soon I had a thriving business. I was very professional: I had all the bags, the packaging, everything! I was out there next to the adult vendors who did it full-time (for me, it was more of a side hustle). Still, on a good day, I could make $100.

I knew I liked girls, and I always had about five girlfriends at any given time. One of the vendor carts that operated near my fruit and vegetable stand sold hot dogs and drinks, and I always took my girlfriends there whenever they came to see me.

One day my dad was walking past, and the hot dog vendor grabbed him and said, "Hey, when are you gonna pay your son's tab?"

My dad asked the vendor what he was talking about.

The vendor told my dad I owed him $144 for hot dogs and drinks. (Like I said, I had a *lot* of girlfriends.)

My father exploded.

"Are you crazy?" he said. "Why would you give a kid credit for over $100?"

And the vendor said, "He talks me into it. He comes by with all his girlfriends. He acts like a big shot and buys everybody hot dogs and drinks, and then he says, 'Put it on my tab.' The way he talks and handles himself; he's like an adult. Sometimes I want to cut him off, but I don't want to embarrass him in front of his girlfriends."

As it turned out, my dad thought the whole thing was hilarious and paid my tab then and there. But later that night, he told me: "No more hot dogs on credit. I'll shut down your vegetable stand if I hear you owe the hot dog man any more money. You make enough with your stand. Pay as you go!"

That was what life in Queens was like.

* * *

But then there was Long Island. Why did that become our destination as our fortunes rose as a family? A story from earlier in my parents' life might explain it.

On their very first date, my parents went to dinner at the Garden City Hotel in Long Island. It's a massive luxury hotel that's been around since the 1800s and is continually being refurbished and reimagined. A very glamorous place. It must have seemed especially glamorous, I imagine, for my mother, who was just off the boat from Greece.

After their dinner date, my parents drove home along Stewart Avenue admiring the tony, three-story homes that lined it. These houses were ten thousand, fifteen thousand, sometimes even twenty thousand square feet. Most had been built in the late 1800s. My father recalled my mother asking with a sense of wonderment: "Who lives in homes like this?"

Flash-forward to my parents' twelve-year wedding anniversary. My father came home from work and told all of us to get in the car; we were going for a ride. He took us out onto the Long Island Expressway. And where did we drive? To Stewart Avenue. My father pulled the car into a big, white, seven-bedroom mansion, three stories high.

Then he turned to my mother and said, "Remember what you asked me on our first date? Who lives in a place like this? Well, we do."

And he handed her the keys.

My mother was awestruck. We all were.

That wasn't all. We walked inside, and my father had our whole big Greek extended family inside waiting to surprise her. We popped some champagne and celebrated. My father's napkin came out, and we all started dancing around in a big Greek circle to celebrate. This wasn't just a new home. It was our "big fat Greek family" home. It was the kind

> Moving your business to a high-end area doesn't mean your profits will increase. Always watch for a mismatch between your product and the area where you're selling it.

of place where on my birthday we could have two hundred guests celebrating inside the house. (My father loved the house, and just like in the movie *My Big Fat Greek Wedding*, he would always carry Windex in his belt to keep things clean inside. I still shudder when I recall his cries of "Strati, get the Windex!")

Personally, I also loved that house because I no longer had to share a bedroom with my brother. I had my own bedroom with a balcony wrap that looked out on the street. It had to have been four hundred or five hundred square feet.

What a great story, right? Well, there was one thing that wasn't so great about it . . .

I moved my fruit and vegetable business to our new neighborhood and set up my little cart along Stewart Avenue. And business was terrible! *Nobody* in that neighborhood wanted to buy their fruit and vegetables from a kid with a cart. There was almost no foot traffic, and the cars zoomed by too fast to notice me.

What was the lesson?

Location, location, location.

Moving your business to a more affluent neighborhood doesn't always mean you're going to make more money. You have to know the customers in that neighborhood. Wealthy people have entirely different customs from those of working people—and one of them is not shopping at street carts run by little kids!

* * *

School on Long Island was the same as in Queens, in that I continued to feel disconnected from my teachers and classmates. I attended a school called Stewart. The principal was Mr. Cox, and the vice principal was Mr. Brady.

When I was eleven or so, my teachers finally called a meeting with my parents to tell them that they were concerned about my performance. They thought I might have learning disabilities.

(I have since learned that I do, in fact, have ADHD. But this is not always a setback. The lesson of ADHD is that it's actually an asset if you know how to use it; a lot of Fortune 1000 CEOs have it. It allows you to multitask at a high level. People with ADHD can do really well if a problem is intriguing to them and can tackle it with all their energy and see it through to the bitter end. The flip side is that if something isn't engaging, it's going to be very challenging to finish it. You have to realize this about yourself and plan accordingly. In my work today, I personally tackle the things that I know will engage me, and I delegate to trusted employees the things I know I'm liable to put off or ignore.)

I didn't know anything about ADHD when I was ten. All I knew was that I was suddenly sitting at this meeting with my parents and the principal, the vice principal, a guidance counselor, and some of my teachers. One by one, they went around and said, "Stratis is fidgeting. He's not focused. He's looking out the window. We think he's special needs. We're not sure this environment is right for him."

One by one, they all said it.

I watched as my father took this in. I knew inside he had to be fuming.

From my father's point of view, I was *ahead* of all of the other kids, many of whom were still learning basic life skills and would have been essentially helpless without their parents; many of whom would not have the *first clue* about how to act around adults in a professional setting.

I know my dad was thinking about my entrepreneurial fruit and vegetable stand, my adventures with him at the Fulton Fish Market, and—more than anything—my work with him at the family restaurant.

After the teachers and administrators finished voicing their doubts about my capabilities, my father finally took the floor.

"Do you teach things here that are interesting to someone who knows the real world?" he asked. "Do you teach how to do business, or do you just teach economics?"

I remember the teachers appeared surprised that they were being challenged in this way. They hadn't expected that my father would ask them questions about their methods.

"I've taken in everything you've said," my father continued. "I expect you're correct that my son fidgets and is distracted. But he has told me that you teach things that are not interesting and are not relevant to his world."

Then my father issued a challenge.

"This Friday night, I will hold a table for ten at my Chelsea Chop House in Bellerose, Queens," he announced. "I want all of you to come to dinner and bring your partners. It's gonna be my treat. I don't care if you're married or single, straight or gay, whatever background you come from. Bring whoever. Come Friday night at eight and have dinner and watch this kid as he operates on the floor of the restaurant. You will see him telling the waiters and managers how to do things. You will see customers asking for his recommendations. You'll see him giving tips to the waiters on how to serve. You'll see him giving suggestions to the busboys on how to bus. You'll see him interacting with adult strangers he's never met before. And I want you to honestly ask yourselves: 'How many kids in this classroom could do the things Stratis is doing here tonight?' I can't because of labor laws, but if I could, I would make Stratis a manager. He's that qualified."

> My father knew I was *very* intelligent, I just had a different *kind* of intelligence. Never get down on yourself if someone negatively evaluates you according to criteria that are not even a part of your world.

So my father extended this invitation to everyone at the parent-teacher conference.

Only about four of them actually showed up on Friday night, but the ones who did were blown away. The teachers came up to me at the end of the night and hugged me and said how impressed they were. They understood that I was already on my way to being a restaurateur.

My father was reminding these educators that there were other career paths than the corporate world. Not every kid is going to use the things they teach. There are different kinds of knowledge. In certain areas, I had real-world knowledge that was *greater* than that of the teachers themselves.

After that evening, most of the teachers and administrators accepted me for who I was and what I was trying to be. Most of them. There were still a few bumps in the road in terms of my traditional education. I had a bad habit of answering teachers' questions with questions. I would often challenge them by asking if the question they were asking was the *right* question. At the time, this caused many disciplinary problems for me, but looking back I still think it was the right thing to do.

There were other, less serious sides to being the only kid in my class from a family in the restaurant business. Some of them were even kind of cool.

For example, I was the only kid who ever brought live lobsters into class for show and tell. I brought them in a saltwater tank, and I showed my classmates how to tell a lobster's sex, and how to determine its age. I even showed them how you can hypnotize a lobster and make it do handstands. (The trick is just to rub it along its back for a couple of minutes. After that, they become like putty in your hands!)

* * *

When I was twelve or thirteen, my father again got called to the school because I had received in-school suspension. He had a whole new group of teachers to educate about his unusual son.

My father was informed that I'd been given the ISS because I refused to write a report on how the economy worked. The assignment was supposed to be two thousand words, and what I'd turned in was twenty words. Despite being given an F, I refused to rewrite it because I insisted my version was correct.

My father asked to see my twenty-word paper. He looked at it and didn't see anything missing. It was all there: Supply chain. Consumer demand. Creating a product or service that a consumer wants and can pay for. (I don't remember all twenty words exactly but trust me; it was there!) Then my father asked to see examples of the two-thousand–word versions from other students, and then to have it explained to him how they were better than what I had written. At that, the teacher relented. My suspension was canceled.

My father always had my back!

(As an aside, some years later I had to show that I had successfully internalized these disruptor lessons from my dad with one of my own children. When my daughter was just four years old and attending a private Manhattan school, I was told she had learning disabilities and behavior problems. I told these teachers I couldn't believe they could say such things about a child still so young, and that they dared to dissect a kid at such a young age. I really gave them a piece of my mind. Flash-forward twelve years, and this same daughter had a 4.0 and was in the national honor society. These school headmasters and headmistresses are often pathetically incorrect about students. They need to go back to school themselves!)

* * *

As I got older, it became clear that my father still hoped I would go to college. I insisted there was nothing there I was going to be missing. I knew what I wanted, and that was to follow him into the restaurant industry.

He eventually relented and gave my plan his blessing.

Another reason why I knew college wasn't going to be for me was that I'd recently snuck into some frat parties at C. W. Post (now LIU Post). I saw the whole scene of drinking games and fraternity members playing beer pong and knew it wasn't for me. I wasn't going to miss the academic side of college life, either. Those kids could have it!

To give you a sense of just how hungry I was to be done with schooling, I "doubled up" my classes in eleventh grade. This meant taking twice as many classes, but the upshot was that I would be able to graduate a year early. I ended up passing all my classes with mostly Cs and Ds. But hey, passing was the only goal. And I completed all my work a year early.

So I was out of school, finally, and at just sixteen years old. I had never really had a proper weekend off, the way most kids do; I'd always been working at restaurants.

The first thing I did was take two months to go to Europe alone. It was a gift to myself, paid for with money I had saved from working. I went all through Italy and France. I started at the Amalfi Coast and worked my way across Italy from there. With a Eurail Pass, it was easy.

I was learning about different cultures firsthand, and I was learning about food. Every meal was a lesson. Rome. Venice. Florence. I was eating and learning the entire time. (Italian cooking has always intersected with my family's restaurants. However, I think we do a better Bolognese than most Italian restaurants. The trick is nutmeg and cinnamon added to the ground beef. Now you know!)

TAKEAWAYS FOR FUTURE DISRUPTORS

- Defend whatever you have built—ruthlessly, if necessary.
- Don't accept that there is only one way forward on an issue, or only one solution to a problem.
- Having the right product and having the right customer for it are two different things.
- There are different styles of learning and different types of knowledge. Yours may not be the most dominant style/type, but that doesn't mean it's not extremely valuable.

CHAPTER THREE

Make a Disruptor Your Mentor

Just because you're blazing a trail, doesn't mean you're the first one ever to do so. To put that another way: Disruptors are rare, but we do exist. There have been disruptors before you, and there will be disruptors after you. This means that you can find these other disruptors and learn from them. They may have made their disruptions in industries that are very similar to yours, or in entirely different fields. But disruptors can always learn from other disruptors! You'd be a fool not to use this fact to your advantage. In my own life, disruptors who came before me taught me how I can unlock doors—sometimes literally—by looking the part and having the right energy. These older disruptors also taught me about the importance of hoping for the best but preparing for the worst . . . and how important it is to protect yourself from that worst-case scenario.

So, I've just told you about my life as a youngster working for my father, and my experience with schooling. But here's the thing: I've left something out.

I learned things working for my father, and I learned (a few) things in school, but there was another vast area I haven't talked about yet, in which I received a remarkable and important education.

My entry into this secret, other world started innocently enough.

Back when I was fifteen and still in school, I was flying home from a family trip to Greece, and I had the good fortune to be seated next to a garrulous middle-aged British gentleman who told me his name was Peter Stringfellow. I had no idea who he was. (If the name doesn't ring a bell for you, do yourself a favor and look him up. Peter, who passed away recently, was a celebrated entrepreneur and owner of bars and nightclubs, often with a risqué angle.) It was a long flight, and we talked most of the way. He told me he was opening a new club in New York City the following night— called, of course, Stringfellow's—and he asked me if I'd like to attend.

Because I was so worldly and knew about the industry, Stringfellow probably thought I was in my early twenties. The opening was on a weeknight, and I would have to go to high school the next day.

Even so, I knew I was going to attend.

The next night I waited until my family went to sleep, then got dressed around midnight and climbed out of the house using the balcony. I took the Long Island Railroad into Penn Station, and then a subway downtown to Gramercy.

I easily found the club. It was a big event, and Stringfellow himself was working the door. When I walked up, he remembered me and ushered me inside enthusiastically. The interior of this club was breathtaking, amazing. I'd never seen anything like it. For fifteen-year-old me, it was sensory overload.

But in addition to being a great spectacle, Stringfellow's was also eye-opening for me in terms of learning what a hospitality venue could *be*. At that time, my only idea of a themed venue that served alcohol was an Irish pub. But this place had lights and smoke machines and loud music and a stage full of dancers!

Early in the evening, Stringfellow bought me a drink. An hour or two later, I decided I wanted another one. I approached the bar and ordered myself a vodka cranberry. The bartender told me it would be $20. I couldn't believe it! (I'd brought $100 to spend that night, so I paid for the

> You may seek out an experienced disruptor intentionally, or you might accidently sit next to one on an airplane. However the introduction happens, make sure you learn all you can from that person!

drink and also tipped $5, no problem—but I was still astounded. Most bars in Long Island at the time charged $4 for a drink.)

Some youngsters would have felt annoyed or even "ripped off" by the price of my drink. I was different. It *thrilled* me because it showed me something I never knew was possible. I was realizing there were sides of the hospitality industry about which my father had never taught me. The idea that you could create a flashy environment where you could charge $20 for a vodka cranberry was a revelation. And the notion that you could *create your own scarcity* by having a rope at the door was a powerful disruption of the hospitality model as I understood it.

This man Stringfellow was a true disruptor.

I stayed at Stringfellow's until 5:00 a.m. I snuck home reeking of alcohol and crawled into bed just as my alarm went off. I was exhausted, but it had quite possibly been the most educational night of my life.

What I had seen so entranced me that I couldn't keep it to myself for long. A few weeks later I confessed to my father what I'd done. I told him how unbelievable it had all been. I told him how enamored of the place I was. It seemed glamorous. The energy. The vibe. And getting so much money for a single drink!

(I did not share this last part with my father, but the experience also made me question why my father did things his way, instead of imitating Stringfellow's approach. I realized later that it was only my apprenticeship with my father that had allowed me to appreciate the innovation of Stringfellow's model.)

My father was understanding about my decision to accept Peter Stringfellow's invitation and sneak out in the middle of the night. But, because I'd had some drinks, it was around this time that he also instilled in me the lesson that if you want to work in the restaurant business, *you must never drink and drive.* It's something I take seriously to this day, as should anyone who wants to succeed in hospitality.

If you want to work in corporate America—to have some kind of normal office job—you may be able to get by with a DWI on your record. My father explained that if you get a DWI in the hospitality business, *you're done.* That's because no one will grant you a liquor license. In some municipalities, you legally *can't* be granted one with a DWI; the State Liquor Authority won't allow it. And in other states, those in power will use it as an excuse not to give you one.

My father made it very clear to me that I was at a juncture where I needed to make an important decision. But I had already thrown in my lot with the restaurant business. There would be no hope for me if I drove drunk and got arrested.

So, I never drove drunk, but I did go back into Manhattan to learn more about nightlife. After my evening at Stringfellow's, I just couldn't bring myself to go into a Garden City pub anymore. I was done with the local stuff. Manhattan was where I needed to be.

In the weeks and months that followed, I attended nightclubs like Malibu. I saw bands like U2 and The Police before they were famous, watching them play to rooms with just two hundred people in the audience.

I also expanded my horizons and saw all kinds of acts. I saw Diana Ross. I saw Leonard Bernstein perform with Buddy Rich. I saw Philip Glass give concerts. These were not acts that most teenagers on Long Island were interested in; my friends all wanted to go see bands like the Grateful Dead. (Don't get me wrong, I went to some Dead shows too, but I also took in a much larger cultural spectrum.)

A funny story about seeing Diana Ross when I was a teenager is that she was very pregnant during her show. Twenty-five years later, I was at one of my restaurants, and I got to have dinner with the daughter she'd been pregnant with! When I met her, I was like, "Your mother was on tour with you when I saw her perform. Now we're having dinner all these years later, but I kind of feel like I've met you before!"

So how did I—still in my midteens, you will remember—get into all these places? Simple. I used my knowledge of the hospitality industry.

It was easy for me to sneak into venues through delivery entrances. I knew where to look to find service doors, and I knew what people acted like when they were delivering things.

You can go into a whole lot of places—and never be questioned—if you simply know how to carry yourself. If you look like you belong somewhere, then people don't ask too many questions. (And if they *do* ask a question, and you already work in the hospitality industry, then you probably know how to answer it.) You have to come on the correct wavelength, with the correct energy. But if you can do that, then doors are going to open up for you.

> Learn the social currency of the industry in which you intend to become a leader. If looking or acting a certain way will create access for you, then use that fact to your advantage!

My cousin Hope would also help to get me into nightclubs by dressing up as a character she called "Countess Hope." She was known in club circles as a real countess. I sort of rode her coattails into places. (My brother, Nick, who was three years older than I, would also get into the clubs, but he never wanted to take me along, so I always went with Hope!)

* * *

By the late eighties, I was a nightclub regular. Every Thursday my friends and I would start at Canastel's, which was created by famed restaurateur and close friend Marc Packer (a legend who later founded Tao, Avra, and many others). He became one of my favorite people and somewhat like a second father, as he always had good advice for me. (It was different advice from what I'd get from my dad because Marc was in the NYC scene.) Our regular waitress at Canastel's was a lovely, kind young woman named Sandra. She was an aspiring actress. Some years later, when I saw her star in the movie *Speed,* I thought, *Hey, she made it! It's nice when that happens to one of the good ones!*

Not to go too far out on a tangent, but these evenings of nightclubbing were proof positive for me that some people really do have an *energy* about them.

As an adult, I've been in situations where people like Mick Jagger, or Barack Obama, or Donald Trump walked into a room—and I've felt the energy literally change. I can't totally explain it. I know it's not simply the fact that these men are celebrities, and that a room can quiet down when people are pointing out famous people. I'm talking about the energy of the room itself. I've been a student of this phenomenon for years, and it's something I'm still learning about.

As a restaurateur, I can walk into a venue and know if a restaurant or bar is going to succeed or fail within about five minutes. It's all because of the energy. It's the people. It's the flow. It's the layout. It all combines in a way that you can learn to read.

I've been in situations where I could tell that a room in one of my own restaurants just didn't work. I've learned the hard way that there's just one thing to do in that situation: you've got to tear that room apart and start over again. (I've been talked out of doing this a time or two, and every time the room in question has been a failure.)

Reading the energy of places or people isn't something you can learn from a book, unfortunately. It has to be learned from experience. Some energy portends success and other energy means failure. You have to make yourself a student of this remarkable truth, respect it, and learn to trust your gut.

I once had a conversation with my father about this phenomenon of reading the energy of certain places and venues in the hospitality business. My father told me that in his opinion, there were three crucial elements to a successful restaurant: Food, service, and atmosphere (his word for energy). All three of them have to work hand in hand. From the moment a customer walks in, all three have to be right. My father also explained that you have to "bat 1.000" when it comes to these elements. (In other industries, you might be able to get by with two out of three. Say you've got a great consumer product, and you sell it in a store with a great vibe, but the service is lousy. You might still be okay if people like the product enough. But as my father taught me—and as my own experience in the restaurant industry has shown—in hospitality it's different. In hospitality, you have to have all three.)

> Things that may feel intangible to outsiders may be very real in your industry. Having "the right energy," or a similar quality, may not be tactile and quantifiable, but if it has a real impact on your business, then it's real. Period!

As it turned out, this lesson about energy became extremely valuable to me when I went out on my own and started hiring people.

One of the few splits I ever had with my father came about on this issue.

People who are always changing places of employment generally bring the wrong kind of energy. This also tends to correlate with their having learned bad work habits.

As far as I'm concerned, it's *energy* that counts. I've had tremendously positive experiences in hiring when I've gone with people who have zero experience in restaurants and zero education, but have amazing energy, a great smile, and great communication skills. These are the people who work out inside the businesses I run today.

My father was a disruptor in many ways, but in hiring front-of-house staff, he could still be very old school. He saw value in hiring people with twenty years of experience. When I finally started hiring for my own restaurants, however, one of the first things I did was take any résumé that came in with over twenty years of experience and physically tear it up. Sorry to say, but that's what I actually did! When I hired, it was former schoolteachers looking for a new line of work, or kids just out of college. I wanted bartenders who had no experience at all behind a bar, but who were amazing people.

I think the best salespeople in the world are born and not taught. Just because you've been in the industry for twenty years doesn't mean you'll know how to be effective. I want to see energy, respect, and passion. *That's* what matters.

* * *

As we moved toward the end of the 1980s, my father's story became one of transitions. And not always easy transitions. Yet I could still learn from this master disruptor as I watched how he continued to protect himself and prepare for worst-case scenarios.

My father sort of "broke up" with his brothers as far as their business partnerships were concerned. My father felt he was being pushed out by his brother Peter. I loved Uncle Peter, but I was disappointed in how he was treating my father. My dad had always been the leader of the bunch and had always been the one to handle the difficult situations. And for this, they were rewarding him by making him feel less welcome. I never understood it.

So my father thought he was all done with his brothers, Peter and George. But then my dad's brothers came back from a trip to Greece and went to the Garden City house and laid out a plan for them to be a part of King of the Sea, our new restaurant in Syosset. My father was like: "I thought we were splitting up . . . but okay."

My mother thought it was a bad idea, and she believed it was time to cut them out for good. But my father's heart came before his wallet, you might say. He didn't listen to my mother. He accepted his two brothers back as partners, and then he also took on his nephew Johnny, who was the son of my uncle Gus, who had owned a restaurant called Moby Dick but had just passed away.

Unfortunately, Johnny was into drugs. My father knew this but tried to parent Johnny and help him through it. We have thirty first cousins in my family, and my dad wanted to be a father to all of them! That was just the kind of guy he was.

Johnny was trying to run Moby Dick by himself, but he just couldn't hack it. I'll never forget, one day my father went to Johnny's apartment in Washington Heights and found it was full of cannabis and pills. My father tried to tell him that this was not the way to live and further tried to help by sending his own people to help manage Moby Dick while Johnny cleaned up.

At the same time, my father went from having 100 percent of King of the Sea (not only the restaurant, but also the real estate) to having 25 percent because he brought in his two brothers and his nephew. And, frankly, these guys didn't add much value. Rather, my father brought them in because they were family and he loved them.

My father eventually moved Johnny to Garden City to get him away from his drug friends. But despite my father's best efforts, the story had a tragic ending.

In 1990, my uncle Peter told my dad he didn't want to be partners anymore. (I was in the room when this happened.)

My father said, "Oh, really?"

My father had just done another deal for a restaurant called South Shore Manor and had once again brought in his family, including Peter, when he didn't have to.

My uncle Peter just broke my father's heart. He was like, "I want you out! I want to split it up. I'll buy you out."

My father said, "Okay. You can buy me out of South Shore Manor for $500,000."

Peter said to my father, "I'll give you $200,000 down, and I'll give you $300,000 in notes." (To do this, Peter was actually taking a $200,000 advance on his life insurance. He didn't have the capital on hand to buy my father out.)

> Even though he was dealing with his own brother, my father knew what the stakes were and protected himself. Thank God he did!

My father said, "I love you as my brother, but do you think I'm stupid? Without me, you're going to be out of business in two years. The only way this place works is with us working together. And you can't afford to bring on someone as good as me to replace me."

Now, at the time, my family still had the real estate where their Chelsea Chop House location had been in Rockville Centre, and it was worth about $2 million. Each brother had a third of that.

So, in the course of this argument, my father told Peter, "I'll agree to your terms, but I want you to secure that $300,000 against your part of Rockville Centre."

That way, if South Shore Manor failed, my dad would still get what he was owed.

At first, my uncle was like, "What? No way!"

But my father stuck to his guns, insisting his notes be secured with the Rockville Centre property. At the end of the day, my uncle was forced to accept the terms.

Uncle Peter was a charming guy, and great with people generally, but he was not a very good businessperson. I loved the man dearly, but there's no question he had flaws. Peter passed away in 1991, at the age of fifty-seven, just a year after this "bad breakup" with my father went down. Personally, I think it was the stress from forcing out my father that killed him. He wasn't able to keep the doors open on his own, and when he realized that, it was his doom. (He and I had a rough exchange right before he died. He asked me, "Do you think my success is because of your father?" And I flat-out told him, "I do. One thousand percent.")

Just to show you how the implications of a bad business deal can echo down the line, when the Rockville Centre property finally sold, Peter's widow, Dinah, saw that her check was $300,000 less than everybody else's. She was astonished . . . but we were astonished that she was astonished, if you follow me. Not only had Peter secured the $300,000 in notes with the Rockville property, he had also *neglected to tell his own wife* about it. Dinah felt as betrayed as she was bewildered, and she never spoke to my father again.

I think this chapter in my father's life, though it is among the saddest, had lessons for me about going into business with the right people. For one, obviously, you shouldn't do a deal with someone just because they're family. And if you've worked hard to get out of family entanglements, you defeat the purpose if you let them back in.

But also, you need to be honest with people regarding whether or not you think they can be successful. My father had erred by once again going into business with his brothers, but he knew enough to protect himself by telling Peter he didn't think South Shore Manor could succeed without him. You always need to protect yourself. My father did that too when he made Peter secure the notes.

A final lesson, and maybe an obvious one: Be honest with your own family. It was crazy that Peter hadn't told his wife the nature of the deal that had bought my father out. We don't like to think about it, but people can drop dead unexpectedly. Always be open with your immediate family about things that can impact them financially.

TAKEAWAYS FOR FUTURE DISRUPTORS

- **Seek out other disruptors and learn from them.**
- **Open doors for yourself by looking like you belong and having the right energy.**
- **Protect yourself when partnerships collapse.**

CHAPTER FOUR:

Preserve Your Reputation and Own Your Disruptor-ship

As I rose professionally, I learned important lessons about honesty and integrity that every disruptor should know. The first is that no amount of money—and I mean no amount—is worth your good name. The next is that jumping into a deal too quickly and without research isn't disruption; it is madness. I learned the hard way so that you can learn the easy way: "Disruption" never means forsaking due diligence. Disruptors also don't exist in a vacuum. Politics, war, changing tastes, changing social customs—all these things will impact your business enterprise, and they will never stop. You will forever exist on a surface of shifting cultural sands. Be ready for it and take it seriously. Yet own your disruption. In Silicon Valley some years ago, founder *emerged as a necessary term simply to denote the person who had started a business. Now it's the job title everybody dreams about. The same thing is going to happen with disruptor. I encourage you to own that term now. Get in on the ground floor and be remembered as one of the original disruptors.*

Growing up in the restaurant business was like a series of apprenticeships. They came from all different places. Sometimes I was surprised by *where* they came from, but each time I learned something new, it was sort of like "leveling up." I saw how the game was being played at a new level or in a new sphere.

I said before that I'd been working in my dad's restaurants since the age of six. When I turned thirteen, I leveled up to working as a waiter and sometimes as a bartender too, albeit illegally. (You weren't supposed to be behind the bar that young, but I did it all the time; it never seemed to be an issue. If my father was aware, he never said anything about it.)

At South Shore Manor, the bartender I most often worked alongside behind the bar was a sixty-five-year-old guy named Jack McCullough. He took it upon himself to teach me how to run a bar, and he also taught me larger lessons about the business.

There was usually a lot of cash in the bar area, and one night, out of the blue, I asked Jack, "Would you ever steal from my father?"

"Let me explain something to you," Jack said. "If you put $100 in that cash register—which nobody knew about—I'd never take it. Never. Wouldn't touch it. I wouldn't touch it if it was ten grand. I wouldn't touch it if it was a hundred thousand. But you put a million bucks in there . . . I'm done! I'm taking the money and you're never going to see me again."

> No amount of money is worth your good name. If you're going to sacrifice your reputation for a dollar amount, you'd better make sure it's big enough that you cash out for good!

Jack was having fun with me, but it was a serious lesson at the same time. Stealing money would cost him his reputation, his credibility, and his integrity. He'd never be able to work again. So if you're going to steal, it had better be enough that you can live on it forever!

After Jack told me this, I thought for a moment and then said, "What about half a million?"

Jack dismissed this by saying, "Well, anyway, half a million dollars would never fit in the cash register!"

(King of the Sea was sold to Sarge's Deli in 1987. It was never a home run. After the city expanded Jericho Turnpike at the highway and took many of the parking spaces, it was of more value to us to lease the property. Once again, the business was more valuable to us dead than alive.)

By age fifteen, I was booking weddings—and bartending those weddings—and handling upper-management tasks at South Shore Manor. Then, at the ripe old age of nineteen, I finally went out on my own and became an entrepreneur. Here's how it happened . . .

I had been looking into the feasibility of buying a couple of arcade games. In the course of looking into that world, I met and really hit it off with a guy named Pat Martin, who operated in the sphere of games and amusement parks.

One day he said, "Hey Stratis, you're in the food and beverage business. Would you ever want to take over a food and beverage place at my amusement park? See what you could do with it?"

It turned out that Pat ran a basic, meat-and-potatoes amusement park out on Long Island called Partyland, right off the LIE. It wasn't fancy, but it checked all the basic boxes. About seventeen acres, and it had mini golf, go-carts, and a roller coaster.

I agreed to do it and took over a Nathan's-style restaurant he had inside Partyland called The Corner.

The space I had to work with was about five thousand square feet. The deal we struck was that I would pay $25,000 to run the spot, but then the profits would be mine. Traditionally, the park had done birthday parties for kids in this spot—pizza and hot dogs, that sort of thing. It was doing about $5,000 in sales per week.

Now, I haven't mentioned yet that I was a drummer in high school and played in bands. (I rocked a Pearl double bass kit with Simmons trigger pads, just in case any drummers out there want to know my specs!) Anyhow, the first thing I did with this space was bring in bands. I knew all about the big "Battle of the Bands" at Garden City High School. My own bands had always competed. It was so much fun and got all the kids really engaged. I wanted to harness that energy, and I thought throwing a "teen night" with live bands would be the right way.

So I turned the big party area into a teen rock club. It always had either bands playing or a live DJ, and there was also a game room with unlimited games. We featured bands from the local high schools. It was $20 to get in, but that also got you unlimited pizza and soda.

My idea worked. The place went from doing $5,000 a week to $40,000 a week in less than a month.

I was just nineteen years old at the time. This was the point in my story where I first started seeing real money, the kind of income I had never even fathomed while working for my dad for a dollar a night!

So, what did I do with my new income stream?

Well, first off, I bought my first Porsche. No problem there!

But then my eyes got big, and I decided that what I *really* wanted was to go into property development. The ball felt like it was finally rolling for me, and I wanted to keep things going. I dreamed of owning something in the same way my dad did. As it turned out, making this leap so quickly ended up teaching me a valuable lesson—it was a hard one, but one that I'm glad I learned while I was still young!

I went shopping for a piece of property that I could own. A multi-unit place to run one of my own businesses out of and lease out the other spaces.

I thought I'd found the perfect spot in Amityville, Long Island. It was a bit modest but looked like a solid "starter property." It was a strip mall that had four storefronts, and they were all filled with small businesses paying rent. The price was $525,000. I had about $150,000 in the bank at the time, but I could get a loan for the rest.

> People who don't do their research become easy prey for sharks. That's what happened to me here!

Now, most of the banks I went to wanted my father to cosign because I was young (about twenty) and untested. I didn't like that idea. Eventually, though, I found a lender at Columbia Federal Savings Bank who decided to take a chance on me.

The guy who was selling me the property was named Sam Tomiletti. I didn't know it at the time, but he was pulling one of the oldest real estate scams in the book on me.

Put simply, Sam had staged three out of the four businesses in the strip mall. There was a party rental store, a furniture repair store, yoga studio, and Chinese takeout—and all but the Chinese restaurant were fake, set up by Sam himself!

Sam had guessed, correctly, that I was so eager to buy that I wouldn't do my research. I wouldn't ask for records proving how long the tenants had been there, paying rent. Instead, I took his word that these were good, long-term tenants who always paid their rents on time.

So what happened? After I bought the property from Tomiletti—and a broker he was colluding with named Michael Barrone of Locelli Real Estate—these three fake businesses closed up shop after about two weeks. And the remaining one realized it was in a position of power and said, "I'm willing to stay, but I want my rent reduced from $3,100 a month to $2,000—otherwise, I walk!"

I was forced to give in.

It was a rough situation. For a while, I tried to reopen the "fake businesses" myself, but they never made any money.

To end a sad story, I got crushed. I had to go to my father for help. Luckily, he was able to bail me out. We sold the property for about $400,000. It barely covered the mortgage.

But I had learned a lesson that every businessperson must know. And that is: *Always do your due diligence.* Independently verify how long tenants have been in place. Get rent statements. Get the deposit slips. And above all: Learn from my mistake!

When the whole nightmare was behind me, I realized that doing deals can be like doing drugs. You can get a high from it because it's so exciting, but that can mean you're also not thinking clearly and not noticing potential dangers.

Of course, you're going to want to enjoy the high of doing a big deal. Who wouldn't? It's not a bad thing, necessarily, to feel excited about making a big move. But you can't let that high bring your guard down. Always stay on your toes and always take steps to protect yourself.

(I should end this section with a note that Pat Martin, who originally connected me with the Partyland opportunity, also sadly turned out to be a scammer. He had promised me that the park would soon be

> **It can be exciting to do big business deals, but don't get too high on your own supply!**

turned into a state-of-the-art amusement park. That it was really going places! In truth, it wasn't going anywhere. He didn't want to invest any money because a competing attraction, a waterpark called Watertown, had just opened about thirty minutes away. Pat was afraid to invest in his park because he thought Watertown might be his doom. And Pat's park *did* look kind of cheap in comparison. Pat had sold me on all these big dreams of building the park out into something with multiple, hi-tech attractions and rides. But he never did it. He was just hanging on to the park, watching it limp along like a zombie. It was never going to be more than it was.)

* * *

Some of the events that influenced me during this time were personal, but some were things that everybody knew about. Big public events. One of these was the Howard Beach Trial.

Many of you reading this may be too young to remember it, but in late 1986, a twenty-three-year-old Black man was killed in Howard Beach, Queens, when a group of white teenagers chased him out of a pizza restaurant and onto a highway, where he was hit and killed by a car. Four local whites were put on trial for the crime, and three were convicted of manslaughter. A relative of mine, Thomas A. Demakos, was the judge in the trial. I attended every day of the proceedings.

The whole event was shocking to me because it was the first time that I'd been forced to confront the racial inequalities in the places where I'd lived. There were no Black people and very few Jewish people in Garden City. It really was a kind of bubble. The trial had compelled me to think about this, and to think about civil rights. In my opinion, civil rights workers are also disruptors because they are working to bring about the most necessary kind of change, a change in thinking about how we treat one another.

> I was a "late bloomer" when I came to realize how elements like race and class influence the world around us—and that includes the world of disruptors. Hopefully, the rising generation is more aware of these factors at an earlier age.

During the trial, racial tensions were high everywhere in the vicinity. It was not abnormal to see a Garden City cop conspicuously tail a Black person as they walked down the street.

I once confronted a Garden City cop about this and got a disturbing answer.

"Why are you tailing that guy?" I asked the cop. "He's just walking."

"We were tailing that guy because we asked him why he was in Garden City, and he didn't give an answer that was acceptable to us."

I had heard Judge Demakos go off at people who said racist things in his courtroom. At the time, New York City Mayor Ed Koch had been making appeals to racial resentment because he thought it would keep him electable. Koch implied some people of one race had no legitimate reason to be in areas where another race was the majority. So whenever someone came across as racist in his court, Demakos would say: "No American needs a passport to go anywhere in America. Don't be a Koch-sucker." He would actually say this in court!

So of course, I was furious with this cop and made a forceful reply: *"This man doesn't need a passport to come to Garden City!"*

Today, as a successful entrepreneur with two Black partners whom I love like literal brothers, it can be shocking to remember how separated our communities were in the 1980s. There was work to do then, and there is work to do now. There will always be work to do as long as people are excluded, looked down on, and mistreated. And there will especially be work in this area for disruptors, because we are always at the leading edge of change.

> As a disruptor, you will be making change. Always make sure that that change moves the world toward justice for all!

The Howard Beach incident was the catalyst I needed to begin noticing the inequalities all around me. As an entrepreneur, I was going to have to engage with a world that was full of bigotries of all different types. I knew then and there that it was not enough for me to succeed for myself. I was always going to uplift others and give those who deserved it a fair shot.

* * *

After the debacle with the strip mall, I still had the profitable venue space at Partyland. I ended up selling it back to Martin for four times what I had paid. I did this because my father had just bought a restaurant called the Hilltop Diner in Queens, and he said he wanted to bring me in—finally!—as a partner. I wouldn't be working for my dad anymore, but *with* him. That was just too good to pass up.

When we went to open the Hilltop—to "reopen" it, essentially, and really make it our own—I knew there were certain things I wanted to do my way. I'd had a taste of flying under my own power, and I liked it. Not only that, but I trusted my intuition when it came to incorporating elements that would help a business really take off.

I should mention that, around this time, 1990 or so, I had started going to nice restaurants in Manhattan. My father just didn't understand this. When I told him that a friend and I had spent $200 on dinner for ourselves (in 1980s money), he absolutely fumed. Why was I so willing to part with my hard-earned money so easily?

But what my father didn't yet realize was that these restaurants were a crucial part of my ongoing education. They were like my college campus. The things I was exposed to in these places were things I could file away to use in the future. For example, the world-renowned chef Daniel Boulud was exposing me to aspects of hospitality that I'd never even considered before. The things he did blew my mind and showed me what could be accomplished in a culinary venue. (I should mention that Boulud is a personal hero of mine, and my brother's mentor.)

When it came to our plans for the Hilltop, I told my dad: "Here's what I want to do. There's a sous-chef named Gabriel Moran working at a restaurant in Manhattan called Van Dam. He's just gotten a three-star review in the *New York Times*. I want to bring him to the Hilltop."

My dad was like, "What? Why do you want to bring that kind of chef to a diner in Queens?"

I said, "I want him to focus on fish, pasta, vegetables, and salads. If he does just that, I think he can elevate the game. His touch will make the Hilltop into a place where people have serious meals. Right now, people don't think of going to a Greek diner to get fine pasta or fish. I want to change that."

Look at me disrupting again! In this case, I was disrupting the paradigm of what a Greek-run diner in Queens is supposed to be. I didn't want to accept the status quo around what we "had" to be. I felt like shouting to the world: "Who says we can't do that? *Who?*"

So after some tough conversations with my father, I was able to convince him to give Gabriel Moran a try. But then he wanted to fight me when it came to the wine list!

I tried to tell my dad: "Look, we *have* to update the wine list. We just can't serve this great food and then have horrible wine."

At the time, my father was fine with Mateus and Gallo on the wine list. They were inexpensive brands, and they came in big jugs. I knew they simply wouldn't pair with the food we aimed to serve.

Once again, it took some convincing, but I gradually got my father to come around on the wine, as well. My father had been planning to keep the Hilltop's existing list of seven very so-so wines. By the time I was done, we were going to offer a selection of sixty different bottles of excellent wine. It would mean working with seven different wine vendors as opposed to the single one the prior owner had used, but I knew it was going to be worth it.

There were other places where I wasn't able to reach my dad, however. For example, I wanted him to install a POS (point of sale) system to prevent theft. My father just didn't think it would work. My father's idea of theft was someone reaching over a counter and grabbing a cheesecake. My father didn't get how inventory management could allow us to keep food costs low and keep everything organized. We could have streamlined our ordering process and prevented leakage. But I couldn't get him onboard.

He also resisted my idea that the Greek diner was something that could eventually be scaled and taken into the franchise world.

"Everybody loves a Greek diner," I would tell him, "and people would eat at our franchises in every major city across the country." My father never wanted to think bigger than one spot. He also did not think we could *trust* franchisees.

"If your mother and I are not there overseeing things personally, they're going to rob us!" he would say.

I tried to explain the advantages of getting a percentage of the gross and having many locations, but at the end of the day, I could never convince him. When it came to this area, my father's own propensity for disruption apparently reached a limit. (In my opinion, you can see my father's missed opportunity in the rise of The Cheesecake Factory, which has many of the offerings of a high-end Greek diner menu.)

* * *

One day, my father and I were in the Hilltop Diner, arguing over my proposed changes, as always, when synchronicity happened!

Own the title of "disruptor." Make it your story. If you do, amazing things can happen!

There was this nondescript guy sitting in one of the booths who'd been there for a really long time. My father and I were specifically arguing over how the poached salmon should be served, and this guy got up and interrupted us. He said his name was Daniel Young, and he was a reporter for the *Daily News*. He said he'd been listening to us argue about the direction of the diner for the past hour. Our back-and-forth, he said, had given him an idea to write a story about two different generations fighting over what a Greek diner should be. He said he thought it would be an incredible news story.

We agreed to let him interview us, and then he wrote the story. It came out, and it seemed the man hadn't been lying. It ended up being the cover story for an issue of *Daily News Magazine.* Suddenly, everybody wanted to come out to Queens and give us a shot. We became the only diner in the city where you needed a reservation to eat there on a Friday or a Saturday. We literally had lines out the door. Overnight, our business doubled!

This made my father trust me even more. Soon, he put me in charge of operations, and he let me use this as an opportunity to really clean house.

To give just one example, there was a chef named George who worked at the Hilltop. He'd been with my father off and on for about thirty years. I'd heard through the grapevine that George was stealing, but when I brought it up, my father had always insisted, "George would *never* steal from us. He's been loyal for years." But after I'd proved how my methods could double our business at the Hilltop, my father said, "Okay, check it out."

One night, on my day off, I hung out at the gas station across the street from the Hilltop, just watching. I stayed there the entire evening.

Periodically, I'd see George step outside to throw garbage away. That was odd. I thought: "Now why would George be the one to take out the trash? He's the chef."

George clocked out at about 11:00 p.m. that night. Around 11:45, I saw him outside returning to the garbage can and opening a bag. I moved closer to get a look.

Even from a distance, I could see that inside the bag he's got things wrapped in tinfoil. He started to remove the tinfoil items and put them into a separate bag. I ran up and grabbed him from behind. I ripped the bag out of his hand and started to go through it. It contained lobster tails, shrimp, steaks, and scallops—all wrapped in tinfoil.

I used this as leverage with my father, yet again, to show him that I could bring valuable changes to the business. I wasn't trying to rub it in, but I told him, "George was here for thirty years, and who knows how long he was stealing from you? I put a stop to it after being here just a few weeks."

My father took the point.

We estimated George had been stealing around $1,000 worth of food a week, on top of his salary (and we paid him a good salary). I had just saved our business all that money.

After the incident with George, it was clear to my dad that I wasn't going to treat him like his brothers had. Instead, I was going to break a few eggs, so to speak, in order to protect us. I was going to look for new efficiencies and better ways to do business. And when people needed to update their skills, I would retrain them.

I ended up retraining people at the Hilltop who had worked for my father for twenty or thirty years. I did it over and over when I had to. I helped them to get rid of bad habits and to learn better ones. And the business was never the same!

TAKEAWAYS FOR FUTURE DISRUPTORS

- **No amount of money is worth your good name.**
- **Always do your research before you jump into a deal.**
- **You exist in an ever-changing world; act like it.**
- **Own the title of "disruptor" and make disruption your story . . . and wonderful things can happen!**

CHAPTER FIVE:

Partner with Whoever You Think Will Help You

There are perceived ideas and stereotypes about who businesspeople should build partnerships with, and who they should avoid. There are also stereotypes about people connected to organized crime families. When I ventured into the Manhattan hospitality business, I found myself going against the traditional wisdom when it came to who I associated with. But you know what? I've never made a better choice. I gave the people around me a chance to show me who they really were. When I did this, everything changed. I learned that mobsters could be far more honorable than Ivy League MBAs, and that many stereotypes had been created by people with their own agenda. By disrupting the notions of partnership and association, I was able to create a successful business within a very difficult environment. But that's not to say there weren't a few bumps along the way . . .

In 1992, I took a trip to San Francisco. My brother was working as a chef at a restaurant called Tra Vigne in Napa Valley. I'd gone to visit him, but while I was in the Bay Area, I also went to Fog City Diner in San Francisco. I was blown away by what I saw.

Fog City Diner was a classic 1930s-style diner near the Embarcadero. It had a great stainless-steel interior, a tremendously cool vibe, and even better food than what we were serving at the Hilltop. It also had a proper oyster bar, which was amazing to me. You just didn't see that inside a diner.

So what did I do when I got back to the East Coast? I created a new restaurant venue called Gotham City Diner.

Located at Eighty-first and Second Avenue, it was my first foray into Manhattan. My dad had nothing to do with this venture; it was all me. I was once again feeling infallible. After what I'd done at Hilltop, I knew I was back on a hot streak.

Gotham City Diner had a metallic-style interior like Fog City Diner's, but there were also differences. It was a New York place through and through. The decor and style were all East Coast. The week of the grand opening, I even had a spotlight flashing the "Bat Signal" from Batman in the sky overhead.

Gotham City Diner did great from the get-go. We were always packed. It served breakfast starting at 8:00 a.m., and in the evenings it became a nightclub that went until five in the morning. I hired Mark Ronson as a DJ. We soon had regulars who came night after night, and we all became friends. As it turned

> **My connected regulars at Gotham City Diner changed my mind about people in the life. By being open to this association and not listening to stereotypes, I would create opportunities for myself in the future.**

out, a lot of those regulars I hit it off with just so happened to be the new generation in power in the Genovese family of the New York mob.

You might have heard of some of these guys: Ralph Coppola. Bobby "Bucky" Carbone. "Barney" Bellomo. Jamie Delio.

And to make one thing very clear, these people became my friends. They never engaged in stereotypical mob-style behavior at my place. They were just customers. They always paid their checks, and they never expected anything from me.

While Carlo Gambino had been a regular at my dad's restaurant when I was a kid and had always been friendly and kind to me, I also knew there could be another side to these things. The other prominent mob memory from my childhood was in 1976, when my father received notice from the FBI that there was going to be "a shootout" in the Chelsea Chop House in Bellerose. It turned out that a rogue group of gangsters had been trying to shake my dad down, and he'd refused to pay. The FBI told my dad the gangsters were planning to shoot up his place on New Year's Eve. Law enforcement wanted to place a bunch of agents inside his restaurant and arrest the gangsters as soon as they came inside. My father agreed to the plan. On the night in question, they came dressed as employees: busboys, waiters, bartenders, and so on, but all FBI. (I'd been looking forward to working as a busboy in the restaurant that night, because I could always earn a bunch of tips on New Year's. Imagine how furious I was when my mother came to pick me up and told me I couldn't work that night! My father didn't explain to me exactly what was happening in the moment, but I saw men talking to my father who had machine pistols, so I'd begun to guess something was up.) It turned out that the mobsters had made the decision to congregate in the parking lot before coming in to shoot the place up. They showed up all right, but something spooked them, and they suddenly drove away. To this day, we don't know what it was. Maybe one of them looked through a window and saw an FBI agent they recognized or saw something in the parking lot that indicated law enforcement. We never knew! My takeaway as a kid was that there are multiple ways organized crime can impact you, and as a restaurateur you're likely to see all of them!

Anyhow, during the Gotham City Diner's first year of operation, I got very close with Ralph Coppola from the Genovese family. Ralph would call me "nephew," and I would call him "uncle." We had a close but casual relationship. And this guy was the underboss of the entire family! (A funny part about hanging out with Ralph was that whenever we went anywhere, like to Cafe Tabac to smoke cigars, after a while he'd always say, "Okay, I think we're being followed." And he would get a rental car to come pick us up to avoid being recognized and tailed. I'd privately think to myself, "Avis and Hertz must *love* this guy.")

After Gotham City Diner had been in business for over a year, we started focusing more on the nightlife events. At the time, our evening entertainment was being promoted by Noel Ashman, a very successful nightclub promoter. When we did things right, we had the place running nearly twenty-four hours; right when the last of the nightlife people were calling it quits, the diner was starting to serve breakfast. It was a great balance. Everything was going gangbusters.

Then it happened.

One night I walked out of Gotham City Diner, and right outside I ran into Ashman—and he had a fresh bloody nose. Bright red blood everywhere.

I'm like, "What's going on? What happened to you?"

What had happened?

John Gotti Jr. had happened.

After his dad had been sent to prison, John Gotti Jr. was made—at least nominally—the head of the Gambino crime family. (Promoting

John Jr. to replace his father was a controversial move within the world of La Cosa Nostra, to say the least, but that's a whole other story!) The Gambinos were generally regarded as the second most powerful family at the time, behind only the Genovese family.

Just to give you a sense of what a jerk John Jr. was, one night I was relaxing at Sprats on the Water, a nightclub on Long Island, and John Jr. was there drinking with a couple of guys from his crew. (I was there because my cousin Billy was bartending.) There was another guy sitting with his wife

> While my Genovese friends went against the worst stereotypes of mobsters, John Jr. gleefully lived them to the fullest. Within every group there are sub-groups and divisions.

at a table. At one point, the guy gets up to use the men's room. The moment he's out of sight, John Jr. and his friends slide over and start to hit on the young lady. The guy comes back from the bathroom and tries to be cool about it. He just said, "Hey guys, no hard feelings, but this is my wife." He did everything right. But what happens? John Jr. and his friends start to give this guy a violent beating, right then and there. This guy had done nothing but say that the woman was his wife.

By the end of it, the guy's face was swollen and bloody. (To my knowledge, at least one owner of Sprats was a convicted felon, and I'd always wondered how in the hell they'd managed to get a liquor license. The word on the street was always that they paid US Senator Al D'Amato, who was rumored to be a close friend of Sprats owner Phil Basile, to walk through the licenses for them.) No one intervened because they knew who John Jr.'s father was. John Jr. was untouchable in the eyes of many, and he damn sure knew it.

This was the kind of Wild West corruption we were dealing with in the New York hospitality industry. In a time and place where so many people were corrupt and on the take, a guy like John Jr. could act like a cowboy with nobody around to stop him.

Anyhow, looking at Ashman's bloody nose was how I found out that in addition to tooling up loving husbands out on Long Island, John Jr. had also decided he owned the whole Upper East Side night-life industry, starting with Scores and running all the way up the side of Manhattan. John Jr. and his thug friends were going to shake down every bar or nightclub that was making money.

Unfortunately for me, it was no secret that Gotham City Diner was doing well as far as alcohol was concerned, and now John Jr. had come to collect.

Even though I knew John Jr. was a lout, the fact that Ashman had been targeted really threw me for a loop. Growing up, the connected guys had always been respectful and kind. As a kid, I'd idolized these men. And now as an adult, the Genovese family members who liked Gotham City Diner had literally become my friends.

But Ashman being targeted made me see the other side. They beat up Ashman preemptively to send a message to me. It turned out they wanted $10,000 a month in protection money.

So what did I do?

I told them a big "Fuck you!" and said I wasn't going to pay.

They responded by throwing black paint all over the windows of the diner. Night after night, they did this. The message was "Pay us, or soon we're gonna start *breaking* the windows." It could have been worse, but it was still frustrating.

Meanwhile, Ashman's father, a prominent and successful dentist, hired two security guards to protect his son twenty-four hours a day. At the time, Noel Ashman was not just promoting for us, but for all the biggest clubs in New York—The Tunnel, Danceteria, and Club USA. And everything Ashman did, John Jr. wanted a piece of it.

Ashman's family also tried to enlist Bo Dietl to help, but he wasn't able to provide any assistance. Dietl was a decorated cop who became a detective with a lot of political influence. He also knew how to navigate and negotiate with the five mob families of New York, and then some. In this case, however, despite his remarkable skill set, Dietl was unable to get John Jr.'s crew to change their behavior.

So, the threats and the paint throwing continued.

Finally—I remember it was after the *seventeenth* time they threw paint on our windows—I got frustrated enough to sit down with my regulars from the Genovese family. I went to Ralph and Barney and said, "I have a problem."

I explained to them what was going on. They said they would look into it. There was no immediate resolution, or any details on what, exactly, they were going to do.

Then, a few days later, I got a call from them out of the blue.

"Tonight at ten you should head over to Ferrier Restaurant at 65th and Madison," they said. "We're going to have a business meeting about what's going on."

And that was *all* they said.

I knew Ferrier was a Gambino hangout.

I remember hanging up the phone and thinking: *It feels like I'm in a mob movie, but this is my actual life!*

That evening, I don't have to tell you I was anxious. I arrived at Ferrier and was shown to a back table. Already present were Joe Watts, an acquaintance named Danny, a guy I only knew as "Tough Tony" or "Tony Parkside," and others. It was about seven guys. These were all the top Gambino bananas except for John Gotti Jr. These were guys I'd seen around. They'd come into Gotham City Diner and never caused trouble. I knew them, liked them, and respected them. (To this day, Danny is still one of my good friends!) The only one I had a beef with in their whole family was John Jr.

Ralph was also present, and it was clear he was there to be my advocate.

He was very straightforward and launched right into it.

"We gotta get John Jr. away from my nephew," he said to them. "I'm coming to you in respect. *This time.*"

In the moment, this seemed like a stern opening. But to my great relief, it was immediately clear to me that everything was going to be cool. It was all respect. Though he was from a different family, these Gambino guys respected Ralph deeply because he was an underboss, and because he had done them the courtesy of coming to them in this way.

In addition to relief, there was another feeling. I realized I was now "spoken for." The Genovese were saying that they had my back. I was a friend of theirs. I was Ralph's honorary nephew. To mess with me would not be *precisely* like messing with one of them . . . but it would be close.

The Gambinos said they got the idea, and it would be handled. No problem.

Everyone present had a goodwill drink to seal the agreement.

But as we got up to leave, Ralph apparently decided he needed to drive home his point just a little more.

Ralph recognized one of the guys who ran in John Jr.'s immediate crew; he was seated in the back in the group of Gambinos. (It turned out he was the one who had beaten up Noel Ashman. He would also, years later, rat on John Jr. to law enforcement, but that, again, is another story.) Ralph went over to this guy and took him by the scruff of the neck like a cat. He pointed over to me and spoke sternly. Ralph seemed barely able to contain the anger in his voice.

"You see this kid? You tell Jr. . . . Anytime Jr. comes near him again, you and I are gonna have a problem. You better come ready!"

The guy raised his hands defensively and apologized, letting loose with a stream of "I'm so sorry, Ralph! I didn't know! All respect! We didn't know he was around you!"

Ralph released the kid, but he wasn't done.

He stuck a finger in the guy's face and said: "You do something like this again? I'm gonna make you crawl on the floor and bark like the dog you are."

I loved it!

The tough talk ended there. We left. I was impressed that the issue had been resolved so swiftly.

The whole event was also a lesson for me that within La Cosa Nostra families, there can be different groups working with competing styles. I didn't know beforehand, but John Jr. ran with a clique of about ten other Gambino family members who liked to act like thugs and lead with violence whenever they shook down bars and restaurants. They would just go right in and beat up the managers as a first step. The Gambino family members with whom Ralph and I had parleyed, however, showed there was another, better side to the family.

After our meeting, the harassment of Gotham City Diner indeed came to a stop. We never had to pay anyone protection. I realized how lucky I was to have members of the Genovese family as my friends. In the days before Rudy Giuliani's crackdown on organized crime, you really didn't have many choices as a restaurant or nightclub owner; it was either have someone speak for you or pay up.

I want to reiterate that the Genovese family members never asked me for a dime. Ever. Not one of them. They did everything out of friendship. Some people want to say that when you get any kind of assistance from a connected guy, "You're just exchanging one devil for another."

Well, that wasn't true in my case.

Just to put a button on the story, years later, John Jr. came into one of my restaurants, Philippe Chow, to have dinner. He didn't know I owned it, and I don't know if he even remembered who I was. I made him

> Sometimes revenge is a dish best never served at all . . . because someone still hasn't even been seated.

wait an hour and a half for a table, though the place was half empty. He got frustrated and didn't understand why we couldn't seat him. After a while, he started yelling: "What the fuck is this? Why am I waiting for a table?" He never put two and two together. I certainly wasn't going to be the one to help him out by going up to him and telling him who I was. Watching him sit there and get angrier and angrier was more fun!

I must say, there seems to be a movement now to rewrite history, and to portray the Gottis as the "good guy gangsters." The horrible film Travolta did may be part of this. But from what I saw firsthand, I know that's not accurate when it comes to John Jr. He always behaved like a thug and a piece of scum. He's done things that should have seen him put him away for twenty-five years. And other mobsters don't like John Jr., either. His big mouth and his greed and his narcissism make every connected guy look bad.

* * *

For a while, Gotham City Diner had an overnight manager named Angelo. He would finish out the shift that went until five in the morning, then he'd sleep in a booth for a couple of hours and open up the place for breakfast at eight.

One day I got a call from Angelo at about seven. He was freaked out.

"Hey," he said, "we got robbed last night. All the money in the safe is gone!"

"What do you mean?" I asked.

"I don't know what more to tell you," he said. "We got robbed. All $30,000 that was in the safe is gone. All of it. I was in the office, and I look over and the safe is hanging open. And everything's gone from inside."

I told him I would be by to investigate.

Before I'd even hung up the phone, I knew that something fishy was going on. I was the only one with the combination to the safe. Angelo never used it. He was correct that the safe had contained about thirty grand, but how could he have known that if he'd simply encountered an open, empty safe? He was not involved in moving cash in and out.

I got to the restaurant and called the police. As I looked around, I continued to feel that Angelo's story did not make sense.

There was no sign of a break-in, and our security cameras had been turned off.

According to Angelo, what must have happened was that while he was taking his nightly nap in a booth, someone snuck in through the kitchen door, disabled the cameras, and stole the money out of the safe. Maybe, he suggested, the safe door had been accidentally left ajar.

But I knew I had locked the safe, and I was the only person with the combination.

Immediately, I began to suspect Angelo.

I hadn't written the safe combination down anywhere, but as I thought on it, I began to recall situations in which I had opened the safe while Angelo was standing nearby. It suddenly seemed reasonable that he could have looked over my shoulder as I did this and committed the combination to memory.

The police, of course, were no help. I immediately hired an ex-FBI agent who was an expert in polygraphs. I told my staff that I was going to give everyone polygraphs, but really there was just one suspect: Angelo.

Angelo agreed to take the polygraph and kept insisting he knew nothing about what had happened.

When Angelo sat for the polygraph, as the FBI agent later told me, he opened his wallet at one point. Inside the wallet, the agent saw every casino card from every resort in Atlantic City. That was motive, right there.

Then the agent asked Angelo about the night in question, and Angelo gave his answers, still insisting he had nothing to do with it.

Afterward, the FBI agent came to me and said, "Listen, I've never seen anyone fail a polygraph so miserably. This guy stole your money. It was just nonstop lying. This is your man."

So that night, I decided to confront Angelo as he was preparing to open. I asked my friend Bucky Carbone from the Genovese family to come and be my backup. I told Bucky the situation.

"I've got to confront this guy," I said to him. "I'd like another person there on my side in case things get out of hand. He might go crazy and attack me."

Bucky agreed to come along. (I thought I'd made it very clear that the plan wasn't to get violent. To the contrary, I wanted Bucky there to protect *me*. As I say, that's what I *thought* I'd made clear . . .)

We got to Gotham City Diner, and I asked Angelo to have a drink with me. After a couple of drinks at the bar, I turned to business.

"Let's talk about your polygraph," I said.

"Oh, I passed, right?" he replied.

"No," I replied. "You didn't. You failed miserably, and I know you stole my money."

"I swear to you, I didn't steal anything," Angelo said. "I know your family, Stratis. I would never steal from you."

Bucky was seated nearby, silently listening during all of this. Then, with no warning, as Angelo is continuing to protest his innocence, Bucky stood up and screamed.

"You motherfucker! Stratis gives you a job, and you steal from him! You're a fucking crook!"

"Bucky, I swear I didn't steal," said Angelo.

"I'm gonna give you one more chance to tell the truth," Bucky said.

"Tell the truth right now," I added. "Or else I'm gonna call the fucking cops."

"I didn't do it!" Angelo cried.

Bucky reached down by his foot. Before I knew what was happening, he pulled an icepick out of his boot and stabbed Angelo in the thigh with it.

I was alarmed! This was not what I'd planned at all. I leapt on Bucky and tackled him so he wouldn't stab Angelo a second time.

"Bucky, you can't do that, man!" I shouted.

Bucky and I tumbled to the ground, wrestling. Bucky was still furious at Angelo.

"Stratis, this guy is fucking lying to you and stealing from you, after you gave him a job," Bucky said as we grappled. "This is how things like this have to be settled. Let me go."

It soon became clear I wasn't going to be able to hold Bucky back much longer. He was really furious.

"Angelo!" I shouted. "Admit what you did! Please! I can't hold him anymore!"

And that was when Angelo totally dissolved.

"Okay," he cried. "I'll bring your money back. I stole it! I stole it!"

Bucky and I both relaxed. It was over. We had our man.

So I got the confession, but—stupid me—I didn't handle the rest of it correctly. Bucky and I stood up and dusted ourselves off. Angelo was crying, bleeding, and clutching his leg.

> **Make sure you're very clear with your partners when it comes to what you need from them . . . and what you don't! In this situation, Bucky assumed I wanted him to be a bit more proactive than I actually did.**

Bucky told Angelo he had to call a friend and have the friend bring the money over to us, right then and there.

I helped Angelo wrap up his leg, and I began to feel pity for him.

Angelo was really playing it up and wincing every time I touched him. I fell for it.

I told Angelo, "Look, go home and get your leg tended to. That's a serious wound. Just give me your word that you're going to come back tomorrow with my money."

Angelo swore up and down that he would.

Then he left and never came back.

I never saw him or my $30,000 again. (Years later, I learned he relocated to Montreal with the money and has never returned to the USA since.)

It was a hard lesson for me. I should have stayed firm. I should have gone with Angelo to his house to get the money. But I was just too tenderhearted. I should have saved being tenderhearted until after my money had been returned.

* * *

The icepick incident was a little over the top, but there were other cases when Bucky handled things in the best way possible. When he brought about resolutions that I never could have gotten on my own. Ever.

One example is what happened with my friend Hani, who comes from a very prominent Saudi family. At this time, he was working in New York and was a very successful businessman.

Hani met a girl at a bar in New York one night, and they went back to his apartment and spent the night together.

Hani didn't know that this young woman was the main squeeze of the second-in-command of the New York City chapter of the Hell's Angels. It got back to the Hell's Angel, and as things often do when they're passed through the grapevine, it got blown up from a one-night stand into her having a long and torrid affair with this Saudi.

The Hell's Angel put out the word that he was going to do something. Soon thereafter, he found Hani at a nightclub, broke a bottle over the bar, and went after him. Only due to the good luck of having been standing right next to nightclub security, who jumped in and broke it up, was Hani saved.

After that, Hani came to me and asked if I knew anybody who could help him with the situation. I replied that, actually, I did. This was because the Hell's Angels are very close with the Genovese.

Bucky and Chuck Zito, the head of the Hell's Angels at the time, arranged for a sit-down with me and the Hell's Angel at Spy Bar on Greene Street.

Bucky was very upfront. However, I'd also learned my lesson from the incident with Angelo and made sure Bucky knew I wanted this settled with words.

"Hey, we know what this guy did," Bucky said to the Hell's Angel. "But you gotta admit that your girlfriend was involved, too. He didn't know that she was with you, and she never told him. What do you expect a guy to do when he doesn't know? We need this squashed because Hani is very dear friends with our Golden Greek."

That made me smile. Finally, confirmation that I had a real mob nickname!

Bucky continued, "We need this to be put to rest. We need you not to touch Hani anymore. This thing is over."

And after that—and a bottle of champagne—the tension was diffused. Bucky knew exactly how to talk to the Hell's Angel to get him to understand our perspective. Hani never had a problem with the Hell's Angels again.

At the end of the day, it didn't feel bad to have that kind of muscle in my

> By controlling expectations with Bucky, I had a good result with tactics that were much less alarming. Plus, I got to learn my mob nickname. Everybody wins!

back pocket. Going to the FBI or going to the NYPD about this problem would never have gotten Hani the same good resolution.

It felt good to have connections that could help a friend whom I dearly loved!

TAKEAWAYS FOR FUTURE DISRUPTORS

- **Disrupt stereotypes; let people show you who they actually are.**
- **Don't bring an icepick to a fistfight! Be crystal clear about what you need from your partners . . . and what you don't!**

CHAPTER SIX:

Adjust to the New Ecosystem . . . and Thrive!

Virtually every disruption involves a journey into new territory. In this chapter—perhaps more so than in any other in this book—I'll share the lessons I learned in my own journey into the unknown. Because disruptors create revolutionary changes, they often face circumstances that no other entrepreneur has seen before. If that's scary to you, close this book now! But if that's exciting and invigorating, then read on! When you're in uncharted waters, you're going to need to pull on the lessons from your past, and on the partnerships you've forged, to come to your aid when the going gets tough. If you can do that, then you're bound to find remarkable success and have wonderful adventures. As you'll see in this chapter, I definitely had both!

My venture with Gotham City Diner was a success, but mostly because of what happened late in the evening. The DJs. The dancing. The drinks. Yes, it was a very good diner by day, but that didn't touch what it became when the sun went down and New Yorkers came out for a night on the town! Gotham City Diner really worked as a nightclub. Because of this, I started thinking that my next logical step would be to open a proper nightclub. In June of 1994, I did exactly that. It was called Rouge.

As you can well imagine, opening a nightclub in Manhattan is an enormous task. You need friends and allies, and people willing to put up a lot of money. Lucky for me, I had these in droves.

I worked with Pasquale "Patty" Stiso, who at the time was an attorney representing the Genovese family, to get my idea off the ground. Patty was able to get members of the Genovese family interested in investing, and they ended up giving me $500,000 in start-up money. The space that I had identified to become Rouge was an existing club that had been called Corolla's and was not shuttered. It was located at 54th and Park Avenue. I just had to change it over and make it my own.

It was agreed that Patty and I would be listed as owners, and the general manager would be Allie Salerno. He was the nephew of Fat Tony Salerno, the underboss of the Genovese family, and later the "straw boss"—that is, he agreed to be the public face of the family—under Vincent "Chin" Gigante.

There was a long construction process to renovate Corolla's into Rouge. But after months and months of work, the club was ready to go.

Just as we were starting to plan a grand opening, I received a call from Julia Koch, the socialite and wife of the billionaire David Koch. She had been introduced to me by one of my promoters, and we'd become friends. Julia said she was planning David's birthday party and wondered if she could host it at Rouge. I thought this was a great idea. We decided to make it the official "preopening party" for Rouge.

I don't have to tell you that the preopening was a big deal. Now, I have about fifty first cousins on both sides, but as I forcefully instructed my staff that evening, "There is nobody allowed in tonight if they are not on the guest list. Not even if they're from my own family!"

The preopening party was on a Thursday, and the club's proper opening would be the next day, on Friday.

Koch being a billionaire and his wife being one of Manhattan's most celebrated socialites, it was a very high-class crowd. Fifth Avenue. Park Avenue. Those were the kind of avenues who were there, if you follow me! It was black tie, of course.

I had started the night in the back working on the food. (I catered it from Gotham City Diner.) Then I transitioned to the VIP room, where I had a few drinks and chatted with some of the guests. Everything seemed to be going swimmingly. Julia Koch was very pleased.

I had a Nextel cell phone at the time, and suddenly it started ringing like crazy. When I finally picked it up, it was my own staff at Rouge. They said, "Stratis, come to the front. You gotta make a call on somebody."

I said, "This is about someone at the front door? I already told you. Nobody who's not on the list is coming in tonight. I don't care if it's my mom."

The staff member said, "No, I'm not doing it. *You* have to come make this call."

So I navigated through the well-heeled crowd to the door of Rouge. I was a little intoxicated by this time, and annoyed I had to deal with this.

I got to the door and glanced at the people in question. At first glance—which was all I gave—I saw a Black man in gold chains and a do-rag, and a white lady with blonde hair wearing a Yankees bomber jacket and baseball cap down over her face.

I immediately said, "Fuck no," and made a cut-my-throat sign, indicating they were not to be admitted.

For a moment, the guys working the door tried to say something more to me. But I shouted, "I don't wanna hear it! The way they look? They're not coming in!"

So the evening ended. David Koch's birthday party concluded without a hitch, and I went home to try to get some sleep before the official opening the next day.

But early on Friday morning, my phone started blowing up. (It started ringing at seven, and I hadn't fallen asleep until five.)

When I answered it, my friend asked, "Bro, what did you do?"

It was a good question. What *had* I done?

I asked him what the hell he was talking about, and he said, "Go get the *New York Post*."

So, I went and got a *Post,* expecting it to say something about Mr. Koch's birthday party.

As it turned out, the party *was* in there—way in the back of the paper. But the main item from Page Six—that was so big they'd promoted it to the second page—was a photo of me when

> Don't be too hasty when you think you're sunk. I thought banning Madonna and Tupac was the end of my career. In retrospect, it turned out to be a move of marketing genius!

I was making the "head-cutting" motion, and a headline that said, "New Kid on the Block Rejects Tupac and Madonna."

That's who I had sent away!

I believed I had just made perhaps the worst mistake in the history of nightclubs. However, at that time I was still just twenty-seven, and I still didn't totally understand how the press worked.

Little did I understand that when word spread that there was a club so exclusive that it had turned away *the hottest celebrity couple in the world* . . . well, everybody would want to try to get into that club!

The fact that this unknown "Stratis guy" was rejecting music royalty made people wonder who the hell I was.

So not only was I suddenly a man of mystery, but the club was extremely successful. We had lines out the door every night. Everybody wanted to go.

Here is a lesson: When someone wants something and they don't get it, it creates demand. When Tupac and Madonna don't get in, it creates mystique. Most places would have paid $10,000 just for them to walk inside.

To be clear, this was not genius-level marketing on my part. This was dumb luck. If I'd known who they were, I would have taken them to my personal

| **Dumb luck is still luck!** |

table at the back of Rouge and hung out with them all night. I just didn't notice who they were. (The only celebrity I knew at the time was Susan Lucci, and that was only because she lived in Garden City and my aunt cut her hair!)

Nile Rodgers—the singer and record producer who, among other things, produced "Like a Virgin" for Madonna—reached out to me a few weeks later on Madonna's behalf.

I remember the call because he was like, "Can she come in? Are we cool?"

And I was like, "Bro, as long as she dresses right, we're cool."

I'd taken the call on speaker, and I pressed mute after I said this. My whole office cracked up. Of course I was going to let in Madonna, whatever she was wearing! I was just putting on an act for Nile.

Madonna came back to Rouge a few nights later, and she was on the arm of Sam Cassell, the NBA player. He was on the Houston Rockets, and they were in town to play against the Knicks. (We had a lot of pro athletes at Rouge. The night the New York Rangers won the Stanley Cup, they brought it to Rouge, and I got to drink champagne out of it with Mark Messier!) Anyhow, I greeted Madonna personally. Believe it or not, she started by apologizing to me for being under-dressed before. I told her not to apologize and took her to a private booth and bought her a bottle of champagne. She laughed and hugged me. We were all good. She loved Rouge; loved the music and loved the energy.

(I also remember this night because afterward, I was invited by my friend Mitchell Modell to have a bite to eat at Madison Square Garden with Mayor Dinkins. I showed up late. Mitchell kindly apologized for me and told the mayor not to take it personally; I was always late. Anyhow, I became friends with Mayor Dinkins that night. He was one of the nicest and kindest people you'd ever meet but a horrible mayor—and he knew it. He simply had too many favors he had to pay back—favors that had allowed him to get that Gracie Mansion address. Payments on those favors never allowed him to be really effective.)

But Madonna's second visit to Rouge also ended in memorable media coverage. A few days later, I was getting ready to go to work at Gotham City Diner, and a friend called me and told me to turn on *Entertainment Tonight*. I put it on, and there's footage of Sam Cassell's wife throwing his clothes out of the second-floor window of their suburban house in Houston. It turned out that the papers had printed photos of Sam and Madonna leaving Rouge together. (I kind of wonder if they did it because New York media hates the Houston Rockets!) I knew we'd never see Madonna at Rouge again, and we never did.

(As a bookend, I should note that Nile Rodgers himself became a regular at Rouge. He got to be friends with Bucky Carbone. The two would sit together for hours swapping stories about "hits"; Nile had one kind, and Bucky had the other. Nile was also one of the heaviest partiers we had at Rouge. The amounts of booze, cocaine, and women he went through were inhuman. To my knowledge, he's the only guy who ever had a driver take him directly from Rouge to rehab!)

* * *

Opening a nightclub in Manhattan made up for my lack of exposure to celebrities in a hurry! One night, Oliver Stone and Charlie Sheen got into a fistfight. Apparently, the two had unfinished business over the film *Platoon*, and both were partying hard. (Sometimes, Charlie would come to Rouge with a dentist friend; we'd always joke that he was there to keep Charlie's jaws from grinding too much from the blow.)

Another night, we had to take Liza Minnelli aside and ask her to do her coke a little more discreetly in our bathroom. (Not all of my celebrity encounters involved cocaine at this time, but many did. I must confess I indulged myself at the time. I had never been a big drinker simply because I didn't like the taste of alcohol. However, I found that cocaine could numb my tongue to the taste. I was never a heavy user, but I certainly partook on occasion.)

After Rouge closed for the night, I often held afterparties at my apartment, where I would also see celebrities. I remember evenings with Jack Nicholson, Slash, and (again) Liza Minnelli, as well as Ulf Edberg from Ace of Base. On another night, I saw that some guests had written VAN HALEN in foot-high letters made of cocaine on my table. When I went to sleep, they were on the first N, and when I woke up six hours later, they had just gotten to the second N!

Some of the celebrities I got to meet during this period were not even celebrities yet.

Not long after Rouge opened, a friend of mine told me I had to meet a young magician he knew who was absolutely going to blow me away. I said sure, I'd meet this kid. What was his name again? David Blaine.

Right away, the dude was amazing. Blaine would take quarters—metal quarters, from *my* pocket—bite them in half with his teeth, and then magically re-form them. I'd never seen anything like it anywhere. And let me tell you, his sleeves were rolled all the way up.

Blaine also won me over with this trick where he'd hold a card in each hand, facing me. A king in one hand, and an ace in the other. And he'd flex his hands, and they would immediately change places with each other, as if teleported. When I stuck my hands between Blaine's and he repeated it, the cards would catch against mine in midair. I still don't know how it was done!

I hired Blaine to do roving card tricks for my guests in the VIP room at Rouge for $100 per night. It was great to watch people like Michael Jackson and Prince being floored by the young magician.

And to David's credit, he always gives *me* credit. I've seen David on talk shows where he's asked what he did when he was starting out in showbiz. And he'll say: "This guy named Stratis gave me my first job in New York making a hundred bucks a night."

Hey, I'll take it! (Though part of me still wishes I'd signed him for a lifelong management contract . . .)

* * *

There was an interesting oddity to the guest list at Rouge. I noticed it right after the club opened.

The oddity was that we always had a lot of doctors joining us. Like *a lot*. And they would often seem to give just their first name. Dr. Leo. Dr. Mike. Dr. Bill. And so on.

One night, I finally went to Allie Salerno and said: "What the fuck is up with all these doctors? What's going on?"

Allie said nothing but closed the tips of his fingers around his chin.

This had become the universal connected-guy shorthand for invoking Vincent "Chin" Gigante, head of the Genovese family, without saying anything that could be recorded by the FBI.

But I had no idea.

"What the fuck does that mean?" I asked.

Allie rolled his eyes and said, "It's all the Chin, man."

For whatever reason, they had decided to use "Dr." to denote that someone was with Chin and ought to be well taken care of.

So almost every night at Rouge, we had a lot of doctors.

We never asked to see a medical license; we just made sure they were well taken care of!

(Whenever the heads of the Genovese came to party at Rouge, they always paid with a credit card so there would be a paper trail.)

* * *

Returning to the topic of drugs, there was always a lot of that in the nightlife world. However, it was also an unwritten law in the world of La Cosa Nostra that dealing in or consuming illegal drugs was forbidden. That being said, in every one of the five families of New York, there have been notable exceptions. Made men both used and sold. It happened.

The connected guys who worked with me at Rouge took the "no drugs" dictum seriously. Especially Ralph.

If Ralph found out another connected guy was using drugs? Well, let's just say that that guy wasn't going to make it. (Interpret that any way you want!) Ralph was very strict.

The problem was that Bucky liked to indulge. At the same time, Bucky wasn't stupid, and he knew Ralph's stance on drugs. Couple this with the tendency of drugs to make you extremely paranoid, and there were all the ingredients for a bad situation.

One day, Bucky heard that Alain, the owner of Ferrier—the restaurant where we had had the sit-down about John Jr.—had been telling Ralph and Barney that Bucky was out of control with cocaine.

And to be clear, Bucky *was* out of control with cocaine. We all indulged back then, but he took it to a whole other level.

But there was no truth that Alain had told anybody anything. It was just gossip if it was anything at all.

I walked into the office at Rouge and saw Bucky sitting with a couple of his friends, and I realized they were seriously planning the whacking of Alain.

When I realized what was happening, I said, "Bucky, this guy is your friend!"

"No no no!" said Bucky. "He's been talking to Ralph! He's telling him things he shouldn't be telling!"

And Bucky proceeded to take me through a whole plan, step-by-step, of how they were going to kill Alain and get away with it.

I knew I had to put a stop to this madness. I went and got a couple of other guys, and we sat down with Bucky and explained to him that Alain would never rat him out to Ralph or anyone else. Alain was a good guy. And believe it or not, we convinced Bucky to stand down. They agreed not to go through with the hit. (They were as good as their word in the days that followed, and Alain lived.)

But my God! The effect on your psyche when you realize your words—only spoken at the last minute—have saved another human's life! How often does that come up in the hospitality industry?

To this day, I don't think Alain ever knew that he was a day or two from his own demise. And it was all just the result of gossip and bad guesswork.

* * *

Being friends with guys who were connected could also make for situations with "strange bedfellows," as they say.

For example, while working at Rouge I got to be friends with Mitchell Modell from the Modell's Sporting Goods empire. Mitchell was the first guy to invite me to a summer house in the Hamptons. I, of course, said "Yes!" to the invitation. Who doesn't want to go to the Hamptons?

I joined Mitchell at his place in the Hamptons and planned to stay for several days. But not long after arriving, I got a call from Bucky and Ralph asking where I was.

I said, "I'm in the Hamptons with Mitchell."

They said, "We're coming! We're gonna spend the weekend there with you. Tell Mitchell we're on our way."

I was thinking to myself: These are not two worlds that you mix together. Mitchell is from a prestigious Jewish family, and he runs a renowned business that was started back in the 1800s. And these other guys are in the mob!

But you know what? Bucky and Ralph came over, and we had the best time! Everyone hit it off. Bucky and Ralph were like, "Mitchell, when you do the sporting goods show at the Javits, we got you." They told him how they ran things at the Javits and offered to double the size of his booth for free. Mitchell was the cleanest guy you could ever meet, and he totally hit it off with the most powerful guys in the Genovese family. Somehow it worked! I don't know how, but it did. We all had fun!

When the weekend was over, I remember Mitchell calling out, "Come back any time you want! My house is your house!" That still makes my jaw drop.

I think Mitchell would have been horrified if he'd known some of the things Bucky and Ralph got up to. All I can say is, thank God there wasn't Google at that time. It would have prevented a beautiful friendship!

(I did tell Mitchell who they were, years later. I still don't think he believed me!)

* * *

Another thing I learned at Rouge is that the stereotype that connected guys are meatheads is completely false. Many of them could go toe-to-toe with the smartest business minds I've ever met.

A great example is a guy named Joe Watts. He was known as Joe the German because he could never be made a fully made man on account of his German blood.

Joe Watts is mostly known as being one of the alleged hitmen in the Paul Castellano murders—Sammy the Bull himself once famously referred to Joe as "a serial killer"—but I knew him as the genius who invented phone cards years before they hit the shelves for regular consumers.

You see, Joe had figured out a way to buy a bulk amount of minutes from the major phone companies, and then make homemade cards featuring the access codes so people could use the minutes. He would then go around and sell them in immigrant neighborhoods. This was in the 1970s, way before anybody else was doing it. If there is any justice, Joe will go down in history as the creator of the actual phone card. If the guy had been born into different circumstances and been able to go legit, I think he'd be a billionaire by now. He's that clever.

At the time of this writing, Joe is about a month away from being released from his latest stint in prison. (I can't wait to see him and have a celebratory dinner together at Brooklyn Chop House.) I first got close to Joe Watts when he was dating my general manager at Gotham City Diner, a young lady named Tannaz.

Then, when I moved on to Rouge, Joe used to come there and always wanted to make a big entrance. Believe it or not, he once had the idea that he would come into Rouge while riding a white horse. He wasn't speaking figuratively! One night, he rode up to the door of Rouge on a white horse. Joe wanted to ride it inside, but the horse had trouble negotiating the steps. In the end, some other connected guys had to convince Joe to leave the horse outside!

Joe would always tip $2,000 before he even sat down at Rouge. He'd get a Johnny Walker Blue with a single ice cube and then pay Max the DJ $1,000 to play the theme of the Lone Ranger, or else a Tina Turner track. For whatever reason, he wanted those to be his theme songs!

Joe is a great guy, and I can't wait to see him again soon. When it comes to the more unsavory aspects of his job, he knew what he signed up for. I don't judge on that. The government says he did some things. Okay. So be it. I choose not to be fazed. Every time I sit down and have a conversation with the man, it's like reading out of a business book. The man is pure genius!

* * *

Here's an interesting note I should also share: When it came to feeling comfortable around connected guys at Rouge, or elsewhere in my life, I did have one strange "ace up my sleeve," so to speak. I never thought about it much at the time, but in retrospect, it certainly impacted how I was able to maneuver in that area.

The ace was this: I had three relatives who were prominent and powerful judges. One was on the Queens Supreme Court, another was an appellate court judge, and one was on the Supreme Court of New York. All these relatives were known as prominent people tied to my father, and therefore to me.

So the men in La Cosa Nostra knew that three of the biggest judges in New York were part of my family. I never thought to bring this up, but there's no way it wasn't on their minds.

Barney and Ralph and the other connected guys who worked with me understood that if I was ever hurt somehow, I could bring the arm of the law down on them. (My uncle who was a judge would always say to me: "If you ever have any issues—that do not involve drugs—I will

93

make sure the whole government comes down on anyone who hurts you. But if you're involved in drugs, you're on your own.")

* * *

The connected guys at Rouge always did their best to give me plausible deniability. They made sure I saw and heard nothing that wasn't above board.

At least most of the time . . .

There was one notable incident where let's just say, despite their best efforts, they did not quite succeed. This may have been because the incident in question was so very strange and involved such a strange person.

It went down like this: I got contacted one day by a guy (his name is lost to history) who styled himself as a Jewish gangster of some sort. He intimated that he was affiliated with a West Coast mob family. But I'd never heard of him or his family. I asked around and heard all manner of things. Some people said his family had money from coming up with a famous children's cartoon. Other people said they'd heard his family owned a big liquor business in L.A.

So, I thought, okay, let's meet. I wonder what he wants! (At that time, it wasn't so odd for people to request a meeting with me for all variety of reasons.)

I arranged for The Jewish Gangster to come and see me in my office at Rouge. The guy shows up, and he's really playing the part . . . maybe a little too hard. He looked like photos I'd seen of Bugsy Seigel. Like a guy trying to be a gangster from a couple of generations prior.

So we sat down and poured some drinks.

"Looks like you've got a really nice business here," he said.

"Respectfully, what can I do for you? I don't even know why I'm sitting with you."

"I'm gonna tell you why right now," he said.

He took out a pen. As I watched, he wrote, "10K a month" on a napkin. Then he reached into his pocket, where he's got a pistol. He popped out a single bullet. He pushed the napkin and the single bullet over to me.

"Pick one," he says.

"Really?" I said instinctively. "We're gonna go there?"

"Hey, you don't wanna fuck with me," he said. "Pick one. I need an answer by tomorrow."

I was really dumbfounded. Who *was* this guy, and who did he think *I* was? Would you really try to shake a guy down without doing the kind of basic research that would show he had partnerships with the Genovese?

Like I say, dumbfounded.

I told The Jewish Gangster I couldn't give him an immediate "yes or no" because I didn't have that kind of power. I would have to clear an agreement of that size with my partners. The Jewish Gangster said that would be fine, as long as I got back to him within a day.

The moment the guy left, I went to Ralph. Ralph took the information and went away (I believe to talk with other Genovese family members). Then he quickly came back with a reply.

"Stratis," Ralph said, "make the appointment. Tell him you're going to pay the ten thousand. And tell him you want to meet with him to celebrate our new relationship at Rouge, late tomorrow night."

So I called The Jewish Gangster and let him know. Friday. Rouge. Midnight. We got a deal.

The guy showed up the next night at midnight. I took him to a table where Ralph already was, and we all sat down. I explained to The Jewish Gangster that Ralph was my partner.

Ralph was very charming. He said to me, "Nephew, I'll take it from here."

I left Ralph and the guy alone in our private VIP room. It was a crowded night at the club, and I had a lot to do. But I returned about half an hour later, and to my surprise they were laughing and celebrating. They were popping champagne and carrying on like old friends.

I took Bucky aside and said, "What the fuck is going on here? Am I seeing this correctly? Why is Ralph making friends with this guy who fucking threatened my life with a bullet?"

Bucky had no answer for me. I was confused by Ralph's hospitality, and I was getting more and more pissed off by the moment!

I left the VIP area and came back near closing time, at about five in the morning. They were still there. Still carrying on.

I was like, "Just checking in, fellas. Everything good?"

Ralph looked up at me and said, "Nephew, we're having a great time."

So I turned to leave. As I neared the door, I heard Ralph say to The Jewish Gangster, "Okay, we had a good time. Now let's talk nitty-gritty. Here's my counteroffer . . ."

I glanced back over my shoulder and saw that Ralph had picked up a forty-pound candelabra. The Jewish Gangster was very intoxicated and just watching it all happen. Ralph lifted the candelabra like a baseball bat and knocked The Jewish Gangster hard over the head. I mean, Ralph just crushed his face. Blood spatter hit the walls. Ralph just kept swinging. He was a big, muscular guy and must have hit this guy six times in the head. Blood was just going everywhere.

> Sometimes "Don't ask, don't tell" can be the best policy when dealing with your partners. It certainly became one of my mottos at Rouge!

Bucky and the other connected guys in the room immediately frog-marched me out of there. This was the side to their lives they never wanted me to see. (I think they hadn't expected me to pop back in, and I'd entered the room at the worst possible time from their point of view.)

I understood this had been the plan all along. The idea was to get him nice and drunk so he'd be slow to defend himself.

When I was back outside the door, Bucky said, "Go! Get outta here, Stratis!"

I did. I left Rouge, and Bucky locked up the place behind me.

To this day, I don't know precisely what happened after I went home. But I can tell you that the next day when I got to Rouge, everything was spotless. Where there had been blood all over the walls of our VIP room, there was nothing but a clean wall. There was no detritus on the floor; no sign that anything at all had happened.

Except for one thing . . . which I didn't notice until later.

When I happened to look underneath the big coffee table in the center of our dining room, I saw that there was no longer any carpet. (If you wanted to discreetly take a person-sized amount of carpet from somewhere, that would be the spot to do it!)

* * *

Another good story from Rouge involved A. J. Benza, who was a writer for the *Daily News* gossip column. A. J. was dating one of the bartenders at Rouge, a wonderful young woman named Rebecca Soto.

One night a guy showed up and would just not stop hitting on Rebecca. It turned out he was a hitman with a group of assassins called the Purple Gang. The Purple Gang was terrifying; mob families would contract with them to do hits. This guy had done time and had a lot of bodies on him. Like a lot. From what I heard, twenty or thirty. So he's just at the bar, and we're aware of who he is.

Pretty soon, his aggressiveness with Rebecca intensified. At one point, he reached over the bar and physically grabbed her.

Rebecca's response was instantaneous. She gripped a bottle of Absolut by the neck and crushed it over his head.

A. J. Benza was at the club that night. He saw this happening and rushed over to defend his girlfriend, standing between the two. It got ugly. There was no more violence, but words were exchanged. A. J. Benza is famous, so this Purple Gang guy knew who he was and how to find him. Pretty soon, the word got out that he was going to be coming after A. J.

> A peaceful resolution is the best kind of resolution—in any situation, and in any industry.

Luckily, once again, my partners were able to step in and clear that air behind the scenes. They made sure that A. J. wasn't touched. Something horrible might have happened, but instead it was squashed. And all behind the scenes from me.

It was a cardinal rule never to cause an incident in a venue owned by a family. This guy from the Purple Gang had broken that rule.

That kind of incident can happen just about anywhere in the hospitality industry. If handled incorrectly, there could be a loss of life. The way I was able to handle it, there was justice and a peaceful resolution. True, some would call this "street justice," but it was justice nonetheless.

* * *

There were other weird parts of running Rouge that I never could have expected, and which didn't involve the mob at all.

For example, I had this friend named Lara Shriftman who approached me one day and said that she had a friend who wanted to interview me for a book she was writing about dating and New York City nightlife. This friend turned out to be Candace Bushnell. The book turned out to be *Sex and the City*.

I had never heard of her, but I agreed to sit down with Candace for a few hours. She interviewed me about what my life was like, and I was very frank and forthcoming. My only stipulation to Candace was that she couldn't call any characters "Stratis." (I was thinking to myself: This book's not going anywhere, but still, on the off chance it does, I have to protect myself. There aren't that many guys named Stratis.)

So I just made up a name on the spot. I told Candace, "Keep whatever you like in your book, but you have to promise to call me 'Sam,' not 'Stratis.'"

She agreed.

When the book came out, it was off my radar. I didn't even know that it had been published until I was watching HBO one night and I saw a preview for a new upcoming show called *Sex and the City*.

> Always be grateful when someone immortalizes you in a literary work . . . even if they call you "Sam" instead of "Stratis."

Candace ended up changing a few things about me and making the character a composite of a few different guys she talked to, but she was good as her word about keeping the name Sam. I appreciated her doing this because there was also, of course, another character called Samantha who went by "Sam," so I'm sure it was a pain for Candace to keep it from being confusing. But I think she did a great job, and I was flattered to be included!

* * *

When it comes to disruption and Rouge, I have to say something about bottle service.

Rouge was *the* pioneer of bottle service.

If you're not familiar, bottle service means that customers purchase an entire bottle of alcohol for their table instead of buying individual drinks. The bottle typically includes mixers and so forth. It tends to be reserved for VIP customers, and it is very expensive. (And very profitable for the clubs that offer it.)

A few places were pioneering bottle service in Europe in 1993. We started offering it in 1994 and were the first location stateside where it was made available. Several other New York nightclubs have claimed it originated with them, but they just ripped

> You may never get credit for your innovations. Don't let that roil you. Just keep your head down and keep working. There's never a good time to sit and pout!

us off! And if you check their sources, they always say they started offering it in 1995 or 1996. Rouge was the only place, and I mean the *only* place, where you could get it as early as 1994.

As we were disrupting, even friends of mine couldn't understand the model at first when we would try to push three bottles on them in one night.

I'd say, "That's fine. The table's $1,000, and the liquor's free. Just think of it that way."

I was thinking of it as real estate. I had liquor companies paying slotting fees to be on my shelf, it was so profitable. (Sadly, ten years later, then-governor Eliot Spitzer put laws into place making these fees illegal. And this guy loved alcohol and prostitutes more than anyone else! Once I ran into him at a diner and stuck my middle finger right in his face and said, "This is from the hospitality industry!")

* * *

One more fun celebrity note about Rouge: Brett Ratner first met Chris Tucker at Rouge. They did a video together for Heavy D for his song "Nuttin' But Love" and shot it inside Rouge. That video is still one of the best places to look if you want to see what Rouge looked like in its heyday! It's on YouTube right now.

TAKEAWAYS FOR FUTURE DISRUPTORS

- What seems like a negative can sometimes become a positive; never assume you're through!
- Be willing to adjust to new worlds with new parameters. Never be scared to be a fish out of water.
- You may not get credit for everything you pioneer. That happens. Make the best of it and move on.

CHAPTER SEVEN:

Make Friends with Change

You don't need me to tell you that the only constant is change. However, apparently lots of people need to be told how to react to change, because there seems to be plenty of evidence that they don't know! As disruptors, we are literal agents of change. We bring it with us whenever we go. As such, we need to know the impacts of change better than anybody. Change is going to come in our personal relationships and in our relationships with our business partners, but it's also going to come in the form of new business technology. Disruptors need to be on the leading edge, but—as I'll show in this chapter—they don't necessarily need to be an expert on the kind of technology that is changing things. Rather, they need to bring their existing subject matter expertise and mate it with this new technology. Finally, this chapter will also illustrate a lesson that every disruptor needs to know: Because change is constant, you must never pin your entire enterprise on any one partner, customer, or agreement. If it should then change . . . you'll be sunk!

In 1993, Rudy Giuliani was elected the 107th Mayor of New York City. He took office in 1994. Rudy started a serious effort to clean up the city and target organized crime. Unlike prior mayors, this guy was not messing around!

The further we got into Giuliani's administration, the more I began to notice that my mob friends were hurting.

And there were other, more specific signs that organized crime was being disrupted. One of the biggest of these was the major fire in 1995 that destroyed one of the two main buildings at the Fulton Fish Market. The fire department confirmed afterward that it was a case of arson. (They'd found obvious gasoline trails.) What I knew, and what later became general knowledge, was that the market building had been burned by the mob. They had done this to destroy the documentation and paperwork inside that could connect the market to the mob. They were covering their tracks.

And it wasn't just the fish market. Giuliani was also driving the mob out of the Javits Center, and out of garbage collection.

Later in his administration, I actually ran into Giuliani at the Havana Club, a cigar bar I liked to go to. I said to him, "You kicked the mob out of garbage, but then Waste Management and BFI came in. My garbage bill went from $800 a month to $200 at first, and I loved you. You kicked the mob

> Change isn't always meted out in the fairest of ways. Sometimes the best intentions fail. Moves that are meant to create a fairer playing field for everyone can have the opposite effect.

out of Fulton, and fish prices went down by 30 percent. But after just a few years, my garbage went up to $1,800. The price of fish increased, too. The garbage company owners were only able to do what they did because they had government help. And they're run by families just like the mob operations had been."

Because they had public money, BFI and Waste Management had been able to take losses to gain market share. They undercut everyone else. Then, three or four years later, when government was no longer watching, they slowly increased prices until they were worse than when the mob had had it.

I said to Giuliani, "Who are the true gangsters here? The real gangsters are the executives at BFI and Waste Management, who are up 700 percent. Look what these guys are doing."

Giuliani laughed and agreed with me.

He said, "You know what? You're right. We didn't see that coming."

So it was the mid-1990s, and Giuliani was cracking down. My connected friends were visibly hurting, and I was impacted, too.

The truth is, I was in business with the mob. There's no two ways about it. I wasn't *in* the mob, but a lot of the guys who worked at Rouge were. A lot of my friends were. And the guys from whom I'd gotten the loan to start Rouge certainly were.

But here's the thing you may not know: Being in business with a connected guy is not that different from being in business with anybody else. In many cases, the connected guys I worked with were *more* honest and upstanding in their behavior than people in the straight world. And the mob was always legit when it came to me. That is to say, we only participated in legal things, like running a nightclub. (Rouge was making so much money at the time, there seemed no need to risk such a profitable, legal enterprise by introducing anything that would be against the law.)

I realized how bad the pressure from law enforcement was becoming in 1995 when I got a knock on my door at five in the morning. It was the FBI. These "visits"—always in predawn hours—would continue through the end of 1996. There must have been a dozen of them during those two years. And they always went the same way.

The FBI agents would knock. I would let them in, or else my girl-friend would. (I learned early on that it was pointless to pretend I wasn't home; they'd been outside and had watched me enter my apartment.) I would always take control of the conversation and ask, "Why are you guys here? What do you want from me?"

They'd say, "We just have some pictures we want to show you."

And they'd hold up a photo of me with Barney and/or Ralph just walking down the street or sitting at a table at a restaurant like Cafe Tabac or Cafeteria. (These were places where we would hang out for hours and other family members would often join us.)

I'd reply, "They're just my friends."

These FBI guys just couldn't understand that you could be friends with connected guys, or be running a legal nightclub together, without being up to something illegal yourself.

The FBI didn't like what they were getting from me (or, more precisely, not getting from me), so the harassment continued. I was eventually called to appear before a grand jury. Patty Stiso acted as my attorney, and I pleaded the Fifth on everything. Everything in court was just like it was when they came to my apartment. They would hold up pictures of my friends

> Even if you're not guilty of any wrongdoing—and you're not even guilty by association—those in power can still harass you when a changing of the guard is underway.

and ask, "Who are these people? Are you in business with them?" I could have said, "That's just me and my friends having a drink in that picture." But it was easier just to plead the Fifth on everything. They asked about 100 questions. I always gave them the same answer.

I didn't like this period of FBI harassment, but it did lead to one amusing encounter . . .

Flash-forward to 2009, and I was invited to an event at Yankee Stadium as a guest of the owner of Grey Goose vodka. There was a ton of security in the box, and they were all ex-FBI agents. I noticed two of the security guys staring at me. Eventually, one came over and just said, "Hey . . . what's your name?"

I said, "I'm Stratis Morfogen."

No lightbulbs seemed to go on for him.

He said, "I know you from *somewhere*, but I just can't figure it out."

Fast-forward to the eighth inning, and the guy came rushing back over to me and said, "Fuck! I know *exactly* who you are!"

I was a little alarmed, and was like, "You do?"

And the FBI agent said, "You're Stratis the Greek!"

"I'm Greek and I'm named Stratis," I confirmed. "But what does that mean?"

"Do you remember me?" the guy asked.

"I really don't," I told him.

"I was the one knocking on your door at six in the morning!" he said.

I replied, "Well, I was the one who was half-asleep or drunk out of his mind at that hour, so I'm sorry I don't remember your face!"

The ex-agent went on to tell me that he'd been out of the FBI for five years. He said the feds had a file on me as thick as a dictionary.

"And we still don't know your story!" he said. "You were always a big mystery to us. How are you walking down the street with the most powerful people in organized crime, and we've got hundreds of photos of you with them, and yet there's nothing on you? We know you're partners with them at Rouge, but that's it. We could never get anything on you."

"That's because there was nothing to get," I told him. "These men were simply my friends."

"Well, I gotta say, it's nice to meet you outside of being in the FBI," he said, shaking my hand. "You were always a mystery. You were with these guys and *really* not involved?"

I challenged him a little and said, "These friends of mine took care of me when I was starting out, and when people like John Gotti Jr. were trying to extort money from my business. Where were *you* guys to protect me then?"

"Well . . . we *eventually* got him," the former FBI agent said.

"You guys weren't there at the time, though," I told him. "I had to do what I had to do. And that's all I'm gonna say."

The guy gave me a hug. He had a big smile, and I could tell he understood.

* * *

A lot of the connected guys I was involved with met hard ends during the Giuliani years. Some died, and some went to jail.

In 1998, I got married at the New York Palace Hotel on Madison Avenue. I, of course, invited all of my friends, which meant a lot of connected guys would be there. Chief among the guests I was hoping to see was my "uncle" Ralph.

During the ceremony, I could see that Ralph and his plus-one hadn't shown up. In the moment, I was really hurt by this. What did Ralph have to do that was so important he couldn't attend my wedding? All the other guys were there, but Ralph wasn't. And Ralph was *my* guy.

Then, after the ceremony, Bucky took me aside and whispered in my ear, "Ralph is gone."

"What do you mean he's gone?" I asked.

"He's gone," said Bucky.

It turned out that the family had called him into a house up in Harlem, and he never came out. Whether true or not, the family suspected he was skimming money off of their Javits Center profits. And apparently, that was enough.

There was a big black cloud over my wedding. I'd really looked forward to seeing Ralph and celebrating my special day with him.

Instead, I was reminded that, just like that, a guy can disappear. (To this day, Ralph's body has never been found.) What made it even more surreal was that I knew many of the men who did make it to my wedding must have known about it, or even authorized it. But perhaps out of kindness, these friends of mine had always kept me at arm's length from that part of their world. I had to accept that this was the life Ralph had chosen. He knew what he'd signed up for, and he knew the risks.

After my wedding, I heard that the powers that be—the bosses—also tested Bucky to make sure he was still loyal. They picked him up in a car, and in the backseat were two guys, Sal and Alberto, who were known hitmen for the Genovese. Bucky sat in the passenger seat.

> When you partner with people who exist in another world, you have to be willing to accept that they will live and die by the rules of that world.

"Bucky," they told him, "you know Ralph is gone. Are you gonna be okay with it?"

Bucky had to make it very clear, in a believable way, that he *was* indeed okay with it. (If the Genovese thought he might get bitter and retaliate, then they would have to take him out, too.) They explained that Ralph had indeed been stealing money from the Javits Center. They asked again, are you able to convince us you're okay with how we resolved it?

And apparently, Bucky *was* able to convince them. He died many years later of natural causes. But that must have been a hell of a harrowing car ride.

I miss Bucky very much. He always reminded me of the character Al Pacino played in *Donnie Brasco*. He was mob-loyal to the end.

Whenever Bucky had had a few drinks, he would tell me stories about whacking people. I would always want to say, "Should you be saying this? Should I be hearing this?" He liked to get convivial with some booze and tell tales of the hits he'd had to do for the hierarchy. He was always killing thugs and betrayers, not innocent people, but it was still bracing to hear these tales. That's how I'll remember him. Loyal to the end, with a drink in his hand, telling me something that turned me white as a sheet! But I loved the guy!

* * *

If there's one mistake people make when they see a disruptive technology, it's that they think they need to be an expert on it—or "get in on the ground floor"—to benefit from it, or even to become very involved in it.

This is untrue, as my own life illustrates.

By 1996, with Rouge now running more or less on autopilot, I was working buying fish at the Fulton Fish Market and reselling it. Around this time, I began to hear about this thing called "the internet." I was not computer savvy at all. I never had been. Honestly, I didn't even know how a mouse worked or that there was a ball underneath it!

But as I got the basic idea behind the internet, I thought, "Wouldn't it be cool to get the Fulton Fish Market online? It could be like Omaha Steaks selling steaks online, but we could do it with fish."

> Pro tip: You don't need to know how a mouse works to use it to make millions of dollars. Ask me how I know . . .

So with very modest internet skills, I tied up every URL related to the market. FultonStreet.com, FultonFishMarket.com, FultonMarket.com, and so on. I had 'em all by mid-1996. Then I made a website featuring the slogan: "From the net to your home." It had a picture of a fish in a net. Hey, that was enough to get the idea across!

Then I learned about buying keywords on search engines. This was pre-Google, believe it or not, but I could still buy keywords on Yahoo and Excite and AOL. I bought just about every fish-related keyword I could think of. I was also canny enough to buy keywords not related to fish but still connected to online shopping. My biggest coup was buying the keywords "flower" and "flowers." (It only cost me $24, if you can believe it!) At the time, I was thinking: If somebody goes online to send someone flowers, I want them to see my site and change their mind and send a fish instead.

By the time I was done, I had purchased around seven hundred keywords, and it only cost me $1,000 a month to maintain them.

Buying the keywords had the desired effect. I went from about five orders a day when I'd first launched my website to more like thirty orders a day.

I answered every email personally. I was the lone customer service rep. I wrote people updates about their orders and told them when their fish would arrive. The whole operation at the time was just me manning the computer, and a couple of young guys packing and shipping the fish.

The business continued to grow, week after week. Before long, the Modell family from Modell's Sporting Goods came along as an investor. They liked what they saw, so I let them buy one-third of the company for $100,000. At the time, I was working out of a Modell's warehouse in Long Island City fulfilling orders. It was about 1,500 square feet.

Then, before I knew what was happening, CNBC came calling. Mike Hegedus, the Special Features reporter, wanted to do a segment about selling fish online, and they had their cameras follow me through the Fulton Fish Market, getting fish to fulfill the orders. As it happened, during the segment we ran into Herb Slavin, the vendor from when I was a kid. Herb was like, "Hey, this fucking kid is gonna be the Bill Gates of fish markets! I know this kid from his fucking diapers!" To their credit, they aired the segment and just bleeped him.

After that, sales went up to about seventy or eighty orders a day. Modell's put some more money in, and we added big lobster tanks and a walk-in freezer to our operation. I even hired my father, who had retired after selling Hilltop Diner (though later the buyer couldn't pay the promissory note, and my father took it back), and he came in and made lobster bisque, New England clam chowder, and all his famous soups, which we then sold as part of our menu online.

It was challenging to keep up with these orders sometimes. Looking for any advantage, I did something that years later I saw portrayed in the Leonardo DiCaprio movie *Catch Me If You Can*. I called up Omaha Steaks and pretended to be an MBA student at NYU doing a presentation on successful online businesses. I asked if they could send me some details about how they were doing fulfillment. They sent me their entire business plans, their SOP (Standard Operating Procedure document), and even listed the publications where their advertising generated the most business: *Southern Living*, *The New Yorker*, and *Country Living*. They sent me diagrams of how to pack and package food in dry ice, and how to cryovac. They sent me information about how to process returns. I could have paid an expert consultant thousands of dollars for this information, but Omaha Steaks sent it to me for free!

Then one day I got a phone call from someone named Jim McCann. It turned out he was the founder and CEO of 1-800-Flowers.

I tried to be polite with him and compliment him on all the success his business has had.

Right off, he hit me with, "Stop the bullshit. I'm calling about a lawsuit."

"Lawsuit?" I said.

"Yeah," he replied. "You own the keyword word 'flowers' on AOL, Yahoo, and Excite, but we own '1-800-Flowers' and the word 'flowers' is part of that—and we bought our keyword first! My marketing department let it go, and we need it from you because it's part of our business. Don't make us sue!"

"Excuse me?" I said. "You own '1-800-Flowers,' not 'flowers.' And you're gonna call me and threaten a lawsuit that has no basis? Go fuck yourself!"

"Fine," he said. "You'll hear from my lawyers."

We hung up. Three hours later, I got a call from Mitchell Modell.

"Yo," Mitchell said. "What's this I hear about you getting into it with Jim McCann? He's furious and says I need to teach you some manners. What the fuck happened?"

McCann had contacted Mitchell Modell behind my back. They knew each other and had other business partnerships together.

"What happened is McCann has the audacity to call and threaten me . . . when it's his own marketing department that fucked up!" I replied. "It was their oversight not to buy the word 'flowers' when they bought '1-800-Flowers.' It's not my fault they fucked that up. For such a powerful guy, McCann has a lousy marketing department. He should hire me to come teach them how to protect their golden goose."

So tempers were high and we were saying *fuck* a lot, but Mitchell decided the best thing to do was try to hash out a compromise of some sort. We scheduled a meeting of the minds, and Mitchell and I drove together to Westbury, Long Island, for a sit-down with McCann.

McCann opened by asking if we were there to give the word back.

I told him we weren't, but that I had another solution in mind.

But I told him if he was going to threaten me again, I was just going to walk right out.

He didn't like hearing that, but he listened anyway.

I asked him how his business was on Father's Day.

McCann turned to Mitchell Modell and said, "Your friend here's a wiseass."

"Why is he a wiseass?" Mitchell said.

"Because everyone knows that's our worst holiday," said McCann.

McCann turned to me and said, "Why would you ask me that?"

"Because I've got a solution for you," I told him.

I explained that the Fulton Fish Market could be his Father's Day solution. We'd put together a package of lobster tails, steaks, bisque, cake, steak sauce, steak knives, and so on. McCann would put it on the homepage of his site and link to us. We'd take the order and give him a kickback.

McCann liked it enough to bring in three of his top guys and have me explain it to them, too. They decided to give me a try. We signed a contract that was only around Father's Day. That was as far as it went.

In the days that followed, 1-800-Flowers automated our shipping system and gave us printers for UPS and FedEx that put the labels right on the boxes. No longer were we printing and affixing them by hand. Before I knew what was happening, two enormous UPS and FedEx trailers pulled up to Modell's return warehouse, where we were working out of. (They had these two giant bays for the tractor trailers. The trucks would pull in and pull out when they were full.)

This was about June 2nd, so we still had some time before Father's Day. But I was like, "What the fuck is this?" Then they gave me the news. We were already up to about 18,000 orders. We were going to be filling these trailers.

This from an operation that had been pleased to be doing seventy or eighty a day!

I couldn't believe it. Modell's knew we would need help, so they sent us some extra people. We packed orders for thirty-six hours straight! Then we slept for two or three hours when the UPS or FedEx trailers filled up and they had to send new ones, and then we'd go back to it.

The whole thing was a gangbusters success. We made about $400,000 free and clear. To show McCann how grateful I was, and as an act of good faith toward cementing an ongoing partnership, I gave his marketing department back the word *flower*.

McCann left the promotion on his website, and for two and a half years we were the fulfillment arm for all seafood and steaks through 1-800-Flowers. They tried us for a Mother's Day promotion, too. It wasn't as big, but we still had about 1,500 orders. Then, at Christmas, we had 15,000!

Suddenly, this guy who didn't even know about the ball on the bottom of a mouse was making over $2 million a year from an online business.

It just goes to show, you don't need to be an expert in a new disruptive technology to take advantage of it. You can bring a business that you already know—like how I knew food—*to* the disruptive technology. (It also shows that you can build profitable partnerships with people you've had powerful disagreements with and said "fuck" to a lot. If there's money to be made, bygones will be bygones!)

> Forging a profitable business partnership with someone has a way of remedying prior interpersonal disagreements.

* * *

So business was booming. I didn't expect that anything was left that could take my breath away. And then we got an online order for $775,000 worth of seafood. Just one order. Charged to a single credit card.

My first reaction was to call my friends who like to play pranks and ask which one of them was busting my chops. None of them copped to it.

I looked again at the order. The name on the order was "Michael Bloomberg," and it had a phone number. I gave it a call and got Michael Bloomberg's office. His assistant told me Michael Bloomberg had tried my crab legs and loved them and was hoping I could provide all the crab for his annual employee appreciation party on Randall's Island.

I reeled. This was serious. It also meant that I had to get my hands on over 25,000 pounds of crab legs.

"Okay, great," I told his assistant and hung up.

Then I went running over to the Fulton Fish Market and told them I was going to need 25,000 pounds of King Crab. In two weeks!

My people at the market were able to pull it off. It was a whole tractor full of crab legs. We delivered to Bloomberg on time. It was such a success that the following year he placed an order for $1.4 million.

That was when Porsches became Ferraris for me! (From that Bloomberg order of $1.4 million, my cut would be about $300,000.) I went from two employees to 185.

Once again, this was started by a guy who did not know how a mouse worked. I just had determination and creativity.

* * *

Another good example of applying preexisting industry knowledge to disruptive technologies also happened for me around this time.

I'd been idly thinking of my father's stories of the old days at the Fulton Fish Market when the ships would pull up to the market with that day's catch, and how the vendors would literally bid on the fish then and there. The highest bidder would take the fish to resell.

I did some looking online as I thought. At that time, eBay didn't yet exist, but there was a site called uBid that held online auctions. I called up uBid and pitched them on the idea of auctioning lobsters. They agreed but said we had to start with an offering of 1,000 pairs of lobsters and offer an initial bid of just $2. Normally, I would have to sell a pair of lobsters for $47 (including shipping and packaging) to break even. If this went badly, were we going to lose some serious money.

I agreed to the terms uBid set out, but I also made them agree that they would feature our promotion on their homepage. As I saw it, that way, even if we lost money on the lobsters, it would still be good advertising.

So we put 1,000 lobsters up for auction. The traffic was off the chart. People were clicking through to our site and buying other things. And the first auction ended with winning bids at about $90 an order. Everybody was bidding and bidding; they just wanted to win!

We made money on every order, and our site traffic blew up so much that we had to add three additional servers!

* * *

But as it goes with so many things, these heady times did not last. There's a reason I didn't retire a fish tycoon!

The first challenge was that when Mike Bloomberg became mayor of New York, we lost his account. No more annual order stretching into the seven figures. It was a tough pill to swallow. Every year after his order, he'd send me a handwritten letter telling me how great the food was and how much he was looking forward to next year's order. I thought it was

> Avoid this error whenever possible! Having everything pinned on a single account is a recipe for disaster.

going to be like an annuity for life! But when he became mayor, we got an email saying they were not going to place their order anymore. Then Bloomberg gave me a call and said things were changing because he was becoming mayor.

I said, "I voted for you! I didn't think it was gonna cost me this account."

He started laughing.

I said, "Don't start laughing; I'm fucking crying!"

Bloomberg explained that a new CEO was coming to replace him from the London office, and this guy wanted to put his stamp on everything and go a whole new direction with the employee party.

So I lost the account (though I still have the four handwritten letters mounted on my wall). I was depressed for a long time after that. I floundered around and made some moves I now regret. The biggest of those was taking venture capital at the urging of Modell's. They had given me their equity back just before the big "Bloomberg bump" and we were doing about $6 million in sales. When they started hearing that I was on fire and had 185 employees, Michael Modell, Mitchell's brother, called me up and started addressing me as "partner."

I was like, "What?"

(The Modells had recently sent me a fax forfeiting their shares to me because they were at war with Sports Authority and Amazon. Michael was always yelling in my ear saying: "All my top executives are now talking about lobsters, when they should be talking about sneakers!")

"As long as you're still in our facility, we're still partners," he said. "And I think we could make that case in court."

"You motherfucker," I said. "You left us alone, and then *I* built this into a $6 million company, and you wanna come back now because I've made this into a success?"

So Bill Modell—who was a legend in the industry, in addition to being Michael and Mitchell's father—came to see me.

I told him I thought what his sons were doing was wrong. He asked me if I could work out a deal. I told him that out of respect for him, I could make their one-third equity go to 15 percent in exchange for a one-time, $1 million payment from him. I didn't want to fight him in court (even though I thought I would win), and I *was* using his facility.

Then a company came knocking offering us $10 million for a $50 million valuation. It was the dot-com boom in full force, and even a website that sold fish could be a part of it! Everybody was offering big money. Modell's rejected this, but then another firm offered $30 million at a $100 million valuation. Again, they said no. I was listening to these numbers and just not understanding it. We were making hundreds of thousands a year in profit. I tried to tell Mitchell that we didn't need money from these investors. I suggested we grow things slowly. Mitchell disagreed with me. He was not focused on profit, but instead top-line revenue. I argued that these internet companies getting these big investments were losing millions each month, while we were *making* money. Why would we want to change that? I asked.

We went back and forth. Eventually, we made a deal with a company that gave us $2.5M for 5 percent equity. With that money, they told me to stop talking about profits. They directed me to spend the money on advertising. So I did.

This connection to television advertising led to an interesting aside.

In 1999, I partnered with MSNBC.com to create a recurring segment called Celebrity Chef Chat. We had guests like Daniel Boulud, Eric Ripert, and my brother. It was a show with these experts talking to guests and answering basic questions like, "How do I introduce fish to my children?" and so on. I had the connections to bring the biggest chefs in the business to this. It was fun and often surreal: we had the greatest chefs in the world talking about fish sticks.

Other things were changing in my life around this time as I got more focused on the online business. I sold Rouge in 1998 after five years—and that's a good run in the nightclub industry.

I sold Gotham City Diner around that time, as well. It had just become too hard to run, and to be frank, I was indulging and partying a little too much. I took my eye off Gotham City Diner, and after seven years of it making money, it started to do poorly. Technically, I sold it at a loss (to another restaurant), but every year I'd owned it, it had made money.

The lesson for me was that there's a limit to how much you can indulge and still handle things. You've heard the saying: "Don't get high on your own supply"? Well, that was me. I was always at Rouge having fun, and I had no time or motivation for Gotham City Diner. My father would stop by Gotham City Diner to check on me, and I was never there. I didn't maximize its true value, which I regret, but I also didn't lose money. It's just that if I'd kept my focus, I could have made a lot more!

Around this time, I got a call from Patricia Seybold from Customer.com. She was *the* authority on good customer service on the internet. She was writing a book about tech companies that provide the best customer service experiences. I learned that, in order, her top companies were Southwest Airlines, Amazon, Wells Fargo, and FultonStreet.com!

I think that a lot of this came not just from our responsiveness in getting product out the door, but from the early days of the company when I set the tone by personally writing each customer a detailed

> **Never underestimate the importance of a personal touch. In today's era of impersonal, formulaic communication, a personal authentic note counts as a disruption!**

email myself. Technology can do wonderful things, but you can't lose that human touch. In the early days of the internet, people were scared about using credit cards over the web. One of the things good customer service could do was build that missing level of trust. You need to make the customer feel like you are reaching through the screen and shaking their hand. You can't do that with a computer-generated auto-response. It has to come from a person. I gave people my name, email address, and phone number when I filled their order. I let them know to contact me personally if they needed anything. That didn't sound like it was spit out of a computer; that sounded like a heartfelt message from another human.

More good things spiraled out from there. I was named runner-up for "Entrepreneur of the Year" by Deloitte & Touche. There was a big dinner party for it. I was also named a Top 10 in Customer Service by *CIO* magazine. I went to San Diego to receive the award and came right back so I could answer customers and pack boxes. (There were no smartphones to answer emails by mobile.)

But let me return again to the part of this tale that is the downswing.

I was doing so well—making money, winning awards—but then I gave in and agreed to take the venture capital money.

Of course, the next thing we know, the dot-com crash happened. I was in debt about $2 million because I'd spent everything on advertising, just as they'd directed me to do! The investors said they were shifting to B2B, and there would be no more money for us. Then we couldn't pay our bills anymore and it was over. Just like that.

In retrospect, it's such a shame because if we'd stayed true to the path of doing it ourselves, the site would probably still be operating today. But people got greedy. They got dollar signs in their eyes and were caught up in the hysteria. When you know something is a good business decision, don't be swayed from that decision. I should have listened to investors like Warren Buffet who knew the dot-com craze was all smoke and mirrors!

* * *

The guy who had helped me develop my website for FultonStreet.com was named Alex DeMeo. I introduced him to Mitchell Modell back in 1997. At the time, Modell had 125 stores. Their website just had the addresses of the stores; that was it.

Around this time, Alex did a presentation for Mitchell about what the internet was going to do, and how he needed to put his products on the internet to compete with sites like Amazon.

Alex told Modell to use his 125 stores to facilitate same-day delivery and pickups, and to handle returns. (If only Modell had listened, his story might have had a better ending.)

Mitchell responded by citing a (now infamous) article in *Barron's* headlined "Amazon Dot Bomb" that forecasted its failure. The article was completely incorrect about its prognostications. (But hey, as Yogi Berra is supposed to have said, it's hard to make predictions, especially about the future.)

DeMeo outlined it for Mitchell: Use your stores for in-person delivery and returns, but also sell on the web. If you don't get with online commerce, Amazon will put you out of business, and in twenty-five years you'll be bankrupt. And wouldn't you know it . . . twenty-five years later—exactly!—Modell's filed bankruptcy. They just couldn't compete with the online retailers.

* * *

So, learn from the past and keep an eye on the future. That's what I'm trying to do.

For example, at the moment I'm creating the first NFT Private Cellar. This will be launched later in 2022. At Brooklyn Chop House in Times Square, we'll be the first to have tokenized NFTs that will grant holders special access to the private area of the steakhouse, as well as a panoply of other benefits and privileges. These NFTs are going to start at $8,000 and will go up to $1,000,000. Backed up by the blockchain, they will last forever, and each one will be unique.

Starting on the lower end, these NFTs will grant you the ability to enter special places within the restaurant. There will be private doors and elevators offering special access from the street, and so forth. At the higher end, token holders will actually own a share in the restaurant itself! You'll have equity in Brooklyn Chop House!

There will also be access levels in between. Some levels of NFT will get you invited to special events and parties. Others will get preference when making reservations. Some will get complimentary chauffeur pickup to and from the restaurant, on up to catering available for private jets out of Teterboro and Westchester.

Being NFTs, there will also be a finite amount available for sale. When they're gone, they're gone!

Everybody in the industry called me crazy in 1997 when I said we needed to embrace Web 1.0. Readers today, mark my words: NFTs. Metaverse. These are the things you need to be

> **NFTs. Metaverse. Mark my words. MARK THEM!!!**

serious about. Brooklyn Dumpling Shop and Brooklyn Chop House are positioning themselves to be big players in the metaverse! By 2025, every major player will have NFTs and a metaverse presence.

I can also add that the digital world continues to hold some of the most powerful opportunities for us in terms of advertising. For example, we advertise on Waze, the digital navigation platform, and because we're located right by the Brooklyn Bridge, it allows us to have a big digital advertisement on the virtual Brooklyn Bridge. It's been the best $15,000 in advertising we ever spent. If you have a small business and you're not advertising on Facebook, Instagram, and Waze, then you're really missing out.

TAKEAWAYS FOR FUTURE DISRUPTORS

- Change impacts everyone—and not always fairly or for the best. But when it's here, it's here!
- When a new technology appears, you don't have to be a tech expert to benefit from it. Instead, bring your existing expertise to the new technology.
- Never pin your entire business on a single account.

CHAPTER EIGHT:

Do What's Right, Disrupt What's Wrong

At various times in their lives, people are faced with challenges when it comes to standing up for what they feel is right. Will they do the right thing, even if it comes at a great personal cost? Will they speak up for justice when others are silent, even if doing so puts their reputation at risk? Disruptors often find themselves in situations where fundamental ideas of right and wrong are at stake. As this chapter will show, you have to pick your battles, but when you do go to war, fight for what you think is right and see it through to the bitter end. Over time, you'll generally be rewarded for taking a strong stand. Others will respect you for it, and your reputation will grow. This chapter is also about the importance of partnerships. Some partnerships can start right but sour over time. Disruptors must be ever on guard against this eventuality. Other partnerships can begin with acts of altruism that may take you to places you never ever expected ...

So, what did I do after the dot-com crash? I went back to basics and opened another nightclub.

In 1999, my wife and I had our daughter, Natalie. My sister-in-law at the time was named Vanessa, and Natalie would always call her "Sessa." So I decided the name of my new nightclub would be Sessa.

It was located in the heart of Chelsea, next to the famous Chelsea Hotel. We had a hip-hop night on Tuesdays. A Latin night on Sundays. Thursday night was for locals. And we had the typical bridge-and-tunnel crowd on Fridays and Saturdays.

This was also the year that Bloomberg first put the smoking law into effect, so everyone would go out onto the sidewalk to smoke. Many nights there were two hundred people outside of Sessa smoking. The guests of the swanky hotel next door didn't always love this.

Not long after Sessa opened, I had an encounter with a Greek American police officer named Peter Triantos. He was a community affairs cop. He came to see me at Sessa on a Tuesday night, and there was no question about what kind of guy he was from the first words out of his mouth.

> **Always stick to your guns when something matters to you. Confronting bullies and bigots directly is the only way to change the world.**

"How would you feel if these two hundred Black people were smoking on the sidewalk outside *your* apartment?" he asked.

"Excuse me?" I said. "If you don't like it, let them smoke inside. I'm trying to obey the new law here. And why does it matter if they're white or Black?"

He more or less repeated himself.

"How would you feel about two hundred Black people smoking outside your house?"

"I'd be fine with it," I replied.

"You're a fucking wiseass," he shouted. "You're gonna fix this, or I'm coming back for you."

I couldn't believe what this guy was saying. And from a community affairs cop, no less.

"I fucking dare you to arrest me," I told him.

"All right," he said, getting out his cuffs. "Turn around and face the wall."

And just like that, he took me into custody. He put me in his car and took me to the Tombs. Let me tell you about the Tombs: it's about the most disgusting, most dangerous jail there is. And I was in a purple jacket and leather pants, getting booked there.

I was charged with violating something called the Nuisance Abatement Law. But we all knew what was really happening. I had two hundred Black people smoking outside in the wrong neighborhood. Nobody would have said anything if they'd been white.

I spent two nights in jail. (When I finally got before the judge, he just looked at the case and dismissed it.) I knew the goal had not been for charges to stick. Rather, it had been to terrify me by sticking me in the Tombs with a bunch of hardened criminals.

Little did Officer Triantos know, but I knew exactly how to work the situation.

Within my first hour in the holding cell, I took the three biggest guys aside—two Black guys and a Hispanic guy, all with face tattoos—and said, "Hey, have you heard of a nightclub named Sessa?"

They were like, "Yeah, we've heard of Sessa. It's fucking great."

One of the Black guys said, "I go on Tuesday nights."

And the Hispanic guy said, "I go on Sundays."

"Well, I own it," I told them. "And any time you go, you're going to sit at my table. You're going to be my special guest."

They said, "We got your back. Nobody's going to fuck with you in here. You're our guy."

Fast-forward about three months, I got a call at Sessa from security for me to come to the front.

"There are guys at the door who just aren't right," they told me. "We can't let them in."

I said, "Who are they?"

"They're asking for you," my security said, "but, Stratis, you can't let them in. We have a nice crowd tonight."

So I went to the door to check it out, and wouldn't you know, they'd all come together.

"Miguel! Jerry! Mikey!" I said and gave them all the biggest hug. I walked them in, and we drank all night. Now they're VIPs anytime they come to my nightclubs, and they don't pay for anything.

* * *

After 9/11, I sold Sessa, and I got divorced. That was a one-two punch. As anybody who ran a business in the City at that time can tell you, everything got closed down and businesses really suffered.

In 2004, I met a woman named Filipa Fino (who later became my wife) who worked at *Allure* magazine. She was friends with the daughter of Howard Stein, a famous nightclub owner. He owned a club called Au Bar that I used to go to, but which had recently suffered a major downturn. It seemed that Stein had fallen on hard times and had recently broken off contact with his son, who was working with him.

Stein was looking for someone to help him get Au Bar back in the black, and I was introduced to him as a possible fixer.

Stein was doing things like "jazz nights" at Au Bar. He'd book amazing artists like Ruth Brown and Dr. John, and they did bring in some crowds (and it was great to watch these big artists), but by the time he paid the acts he was losing money again.

I thought I could help and agreed to go in if it would be 50/50, but, as I said at the time, "I need to know all your debts." He showed me his books, and everything looked okay. I brought in a nightclub promoter named Richie Romero who told Stein that Au Bar had been hot back in the eighties and early nineties, but that the kids coming out of college today didn't have the association for it. So the first thing needed would be a new name.

We went with 58 New York. I started promoting the club to twenty-two-year-olds, and we hit it big. All of a sudden, we were up from about $30,000 a week to $100,000. And that was without putting any new money into the club. (Personally, I didn't really have money to put into it. I'd lost almost everything in the 9/11 downturn. 58 New York was really my way of starting again.)

So the club got going, and everything seemed like it should be great. I was on pace to be making a few hundred thousand a year, which is wonderful after the dire straits of post-9/11. We're not killing it like at FultonStreet.com, but we're all making okay money.

Then I got a foreclosure letter in the mail from SL Green, our landlord. Obviously, I was surprised, but this wasn't my first rodeo. I looked into it. SL Green was saying we were behind a million dollars in rent. I went to Stein and asked him what was going on. I pointed out that this wasn't in any of the stuff he disclosed to me. I also pointed out in the strongest possible terms that I couldn't afford to pay a million dollars in back rent!

Stein's response was "I can't believe Steve Ross did this to me. Ross was my *partner.*"

Many of you today may know Ross as a big developer behind such massive Manhattan projects as Hudson Yards and the Time Warner Center.

It turned out Ross had been Stein's silent partner; he used to own the space and had never charged Au Bar rent. But if he *had* been charging it, it would have been about a million dollars. Stein said that when Ross sold the Au Bar space to SL Green, he put that million on the books as a debt.

I'm still processing all this when Steve Green calls me and asks what we're going to do. I didn't have an immediate answer for him.

Around the time this was happening, I also got a call from Mike Reda, an associate of the Genovese. During my time with Sessa, I'd had a problem with one of my partners, and I'd asked a Genovese capo named Jamie Delio to help me, and he had done so. Jamie ended up becoming a partner with me at Sessa, and he did really well for a while with me there. Then 9/11 and my divorce happened, and I lost everything.

It's important to note that I never heard from Jamie during this dark period for me. Not a line on any opportunities, not a "Hey, how you holdin' up?" Nothing. They forgot I existed, even though they made quite a bit of money for themselves with me.

Now I was running 58 New York, and this call came in from Mike, and he said, "Jamie wants an envelope, every week."

"Fuck Jamie, and fuck you!" I replied. "It's never going to happen. I made you guys a lot of money, and you were never there for me when I was struggling. You forgot my phone number. Now that I'm starting something up you've found it again?"

I had dinner with Mike Reda to talk about this.

After I laid out the situation in more detail, he once more surprised me.

"Fuck Jamie and his trying to get an envelope," he says. "I want to come in with *you*."

This was interesting because Mike had a reputation for taking distressed companies —or businesses with some kind of problem—and turning them around. And I certainly had a problem with SL Green. (An

> Sometimes, all is not as it seems. That's true in business and in life!

astonishing truth came out years later. All of this was a lie from Mike Reda. Jamie *never* tried to shake me down for an envelope. Mike was just using Jamie's name to get in with me by appearing to stand up for himself. Yet, at the time, he successfully got me to hate Jamie. I'll never forgive him for that.)

So I told Mike Reda about my problem with SL Green.

Mike suggested throwing it into bankruptcy. In bankruptcy court, he explained, we'd be able to show that the business is now viable. It's a real business. It's not something that's going to go into Chapter 7, and we can prove that to a judge.

Mike called his childhood friend, a lawyer named Tom Draghi, to see about starting the process.

When he heard through the grapevine that we were considering this, Steve Green called me and said, "You don't got the balls to try bankruptcy!"

Well, it turns out we did.

And Mike was correct about taking this approach. A judge agreed with us and let us pay $50,000 to SL Green to settle, and then we got a brand-new lease.

With this settlement reached, we converted 58 New York again, this time into a nightclub called The Grand. We redid the whole club and had a gangbusters success with it. Our house DJs were the Chainsmokers!

* * *

Some of my forays into disruption have involved situations where I knew there was a tremendous opportunity for another business—not necessarily one of mine—to embrace new technologies and/or take fundamental leaps forward. However, I

> Sometimes the lesson about a person is: there is no lesson. Some humans are just horrible. Period. End of story.

learned that just because you see and fully grasp an opportunity yourself doesn't mean other people are going to.

When the dot-com crash happened, I found a frozen food delivery company called Horizon Foods. I wanted to merge with them and put FultonStreet.com on every one of those trucks. The company would have been called FultonStreet. Alas, banker PJ Solomon's Marc Cooper couldn't get the deal done.

But I was still thinking . . .

I had just written a 250-page business plan called "The Milkman Cometh." I believed that the internet was going to impact the direct sales business via a metric I called "clicks to knocks." I further believed that what we were doing at FultonStreet.com could work if we teamed up with a company that owned a fleet of ice cream trucks, but instead of ice cream we could do steak, fish, and lobster. And the delivery people could go knocking on doors almost like a milkman . . . or the Avon Lady.

Imagine the Avon Lady coming to your house with free samples of things she already knows you want because you filled out a five-question survey online.

I believed the internet should be there to prequalify leads for direct sales. Then, as now, most door-to-door salespeople find that about 98 percent of their door knocks are rejected. The person in the residence doesn't even open their font door to hear the pitch. I thought we could get that to about 50 percent if we prequalified leads using the internet. I envisioned a world in which we would have a fleet of frozen food truck drives making our own deliveries from FultonStreet.com, while also building a database of people who were amenable to be sold this kind of product. We could offer same-day delivery in an area like New York. Nobody was using the internet for that yet.

I had banks interested in putting as much as $25 million behind this idea, but then the crash happened. Just like that, the opportunity was gone.

Knowing this was not going to turn out to be something for us, I later took the business plan and gave it to the CEO of Avon. I'd met the Avon management team after doing a speaking engagement about technology at Tavern on the Green. In my talk, I had been hinting about some of the things in "The Milkman Cometh." I told Avon that all their "Avon Lady" reps could have their own websites where leads could be prequalified, if they were willing to embrace new technology. They would have so much more success taking this approach than they did knocking on doors cold.

Believe it or not, when I then brought up the idea of Avon licensing this approach from me, they shot it down! They just had the old school mentality. They believed, accurately, that their business was based on personal relationships, but they couldn't see how this approach was going to help them form better relationships.

> Some of your best plans might apply to businesses other than your own. That still doesn't mean you're going to find a receptive audience. Like they say, you can lead a horse to water . . .

I was surprised and disappointed. And about fifteen years later, Avon was doing exactly what I had suggested: prequalifying leads online and having their reps maintain their own website.

They had shot it down while feeding me lines like: "There's still nothing like knocking on a door." In a sense that was true, but they didn't want to accept that I could show them which doors were warm.

Avon didn't take my suggestion, and neither did anybody else. If they had, they would have been fifteen years ahead of the game!

* * *

As all this was happening, my brother was taking a very different path from mine, but still working in the hospitality industry and rising through the ranks.

My brother, Nick Morfogen, has always wanted to become a chef, and it was clear from the start that he was extremely talented in the kitchen. He graduated from CIA (Culinary Institute of America) first in his class, externing at Le Bernardin with Gilbert Le Coze. (I should point out that a whole lot of chefs do their externships at places like T.G.I. Fridays. I'm not knocking these people, but my brother was on another level!) Leading people in the industry were willing to give my brother a chance because they knew my family members from the Fulton Fish Market. They knew we were straight shooters who understood what we were talking about when it came to food. When we said this guy in our family was on another level, they knew we meant it!

Chefs and restaurateurs also knew my family could give them respect.

For example, a French chef might move from Paris to New York and set up shop. In Paris, he's/she's a big deal, but nobody in New York knows them yet. So the vendors are skeptical: "Who is this person, and why should I give them my best stuff?" they'd ask.

But if we knew a chef was the real deal, we would make that known. To everybody. My family bought so much fish, the vendors knew they'd better listen to what we said! (Just to give one example, before he passed away, Gilbert Le Coze said that if there had been no George Morfogen, there would have been no Le Bernardin!)

After he graduated from CIA, my father offered to buy Nick a restaurant. But instead, Nick decided to apprentice for the best chefs in the world. That was his postgraduate studies or master's degree. (My dad never understood Nick's drive to work all those hours for a couple hundred dollars a week when he could be his own boss. This changed when my father and mother ate at some of the high-end kitchens where Nick was apprenticing. It was then that my parents truly realized that we had a celebrity chef in the family, and they were never so proud of him!)

Nick found a mentor in Daniel Boulud. They worked together at Le Cirque in the late eighties. From there, Nick went to work at Tra Vigne on the West Coast. Nick quickly rose to executive chef and mastered the wood-burning oven (a big culinary accomplishment—turning it from pizza and breads into something to cook fish and vegetables and more). His cuisine became more Mediterranean, and not merely Greek. In 1993, he opened his own restaurant, the famous Ajax Tavern in Aspen.

Nick was fast becoming a celebrity chef. *Food and Wine* magazine named him one of the ten best new chefs in America, among many other awards.

Then Nick opened his most prestigious restaurant: 32 East in Del Rey Beach, Florida, which he operated for over thirty years.

Nick took the career path of a chef, and I went more for managing concepts and working in the front of the house. (I should point out that I also know how to cook really well, just not quite as well as Nick!)

Nick and I have always existed parallel to each other, and now we're bringing the original Pappas back. Nick is consulting with us. He is now known far and wide in the culinary industry as the master of the wood-burning oven, and I predict great things are going to happen!

I mention Nick here because cuisine was going to play a part in the next chapter of my life, and in ways I never could have expected.

TAKEAWAYS FOR FUTURE DISRUPTORS

- Pick your battles, but always fight for what's right! You'll generally be rewarded if you do.
- Keep an eye on your partnerships. A partner who is good initially may not always stay good.
- Some of your best plans may be useful to those other than yourself.

CHAPTER NINE:

How Empires Are Built

Being ready to get the job done when the opportunity presents itself. THAT'S a crucial element to success in any field. But how will you know when the stars are right? When the planets align? Here's the frustrating answer: You won't know . . . until you suddenly do. In this chapter, I'll share the story of how the right moment came to me, and how I recognized it and acted accordingly. I think it's an important story to share because disruptors have a habit of seeing these opportunities where others do not. Sometimes opportunities come from building on or disrupting another person's successful business model. But other times, disruptors can succeed in precisely the place where others are exhibiting their worst failures.

As I said earlier, I met my wife, Filipa Fino, around 2004. She was just moving jobs from *Allure* to *Vogue* magazine. She was in Anna Wintour's inner circle at *Vogue*, fourth or fifth on the masthead.

Because of this, we attended lots of dinners at Anna's brownstone, and also *Vogue* dinners at Mr. Chow, a Chinese fine-dining restaurant that was generally regarded as the greatest of its kind.

For me, Mr. Chow was a revelation. Walking inside the first time proved on par with my first trip to Stringfellow's. I'd never known that Chinese food could work as fine dining in a white-tablecloth restaurant.

Anna Wintour's dinner parties at Mr. Chow were incredible. I'd see David Bowie, Mick Jagger, Donna Karan, and Rupert and Wendi Murdoch. It was a real who's who, and I was at the "cool table" table because of my wife. I was meeting people who'd been posters on my walls growing up! And not just meeting—before long, I was on a first-name basis with them.

One day I went to Mr. Chow and took along some friends visiting from Greece. I was excited to show them what Chinese food could be, and to see if I could change their minds about it; all they knew was "Chinese takeout."

When we sat down, I asked the GM, "Brian," if we could see a menu. I said, "I know you don't have menus here—the waiter just explains to the table what the choices are—but I'd like to let my friends know about everything you serve."

Brian was incredibly rude and said, "The next time you ask for a menu, I'm going to ask you to leave."

I couldn't believe it! That was the kind of restaurant it was. They had no compunction about asking customers to leave.

The Mr. Chow no-menu system wasn't perfect, either. It seemed like every time I ate there, I ordered the same thing but got charged a different price

> Mr. Chow's rude GM didn't know it, but he had just given me a life-changing opportunity for disruption! And when you see an opportunity like that, you take it!

for it! Later on, after I had poached a few of their servers for my own restaurants, these servers would tell me that the reason for the "no-menus" policy was to profile the customers and charge accordingly. If a couple came in with wedding rings, they would be cautious about inflating the bill because married couples will challenge it. People who appeared to be on a first date, however? God help them. They got gouged, because nobody would want to be seen questioning a bill and looking cheap on a date. Costin, who came from Mr. Chow and later became my manager, confirmed all this for me. Mr. Chow was practicing a style of disruption that is *not* what this book is about!

Anyhow, I was really upset at how I'd been treated in front of my friends from Greece, so I took a business card, slipped it to the busboy, and asked him to give it to the chef. (Nothing makes me more upset than when businesses are not grateful for customers. My mother and father had raised me to appreciate customers. My father used to say: "When a customer comes into your restaurant, they've walked past 100 other doors to get to yours. Make them feel like you appreciate that!")

The next day I got a phone call from Philippe, the head chef at Mr. Chow. In a thick Chinese accent, he asked what I wanted.

I said, "I'd like to meet you for a coffee at a diner on 86th Street to talk business."

He said okay. We met that same day at 11:00 a.m. I hadn't really been expecting to get a call back, much less for him to take me up on an offer to meet. But things were happening!

(What Philippe didn't know was that for a couple of years my wife and I had been obsessed with a restaurant in Paris called Davé. It was a high-end Chinese restaurant on the Right Bank. All the big celebrities and world leaders ate there. The owner would take Polaroids of himself with celebrities and put them on the walls. It was the most popular restaurant in the city during Paris Fashion Week. The food wasn't amazing, but the way he ran the floor appealed to the celebrity clientele. I had actually approached the owner, Davé Cheung, about possibly opening a Davé in the United States. As an entrée to negotiations, Cheung said that he would need to come to the US location and appear two weekends per month, and for each of those appearances he would need me to book him a suite at the Four Seasons, which would cost $900 a night, and then an arrangement of flowers that would cost $1,800 to be waiting for him in the suite. That seemed way over the top. I told him: "My counteroffer is Motel 6 and a bunch of daisies. Take it or leave it!" Cheung phoned my wife and called me "vile" and said it would never work out between him and me. So that failed, but I was still itching to move forward with an Asian restaurant.)

Philippe arrived to meet me at the diner with a guy named Robert Darby. Robert spoke better English than Philippe and was there to help the conversation flow more smoothly. I also got the idea that he and Philippe were business partners of a sort. They looked out for each other.

Philippe said, "So why am I here?"

"I've got this great space on 60th Street and Madison Avenue," I replied. "I'd like to use that space to build a restaurant all around you. I love your food. I just hate Mr. Chow's guest experience. His managers are so arrogant and rude."

"Okay," Philippe replied. "What are you offering?"

I said I'd offer him 10 percent equity, and a 20 percent raise over whatever his current salary was.

He asked if I was done.

When I said yes, he got up and started putting on his coat.

I said, "Whoa, why are you leaving?"

He said, "I've been offered that deal before. I need something a little better if I'm going to leave Mr. Chow."

I asked him to sit down and give me a chance to sweeten the deal.

My mind went to a story that Tommy Mottola—the CEO of Sony Music—had told me years before. Back when he was working as an A&R guy signing artists, he'd occasionally encounter situations where a parent was acting as their son or daughter's manager, and that parent was hesitating to sign a contract. When this happened, Tommy would send over a Ferrari along with the contract, and let the parent know that if they signed *today,* it was theirs as part of the bargain. He said this tactic *always* worked.

Philippe sat back down, and I told him, "How about this. . . We do 10 percent equity, a 20 percent raise . . . *and* tomorrow I take you to my favorite Porsche dealer and let you pick out any car you want?"

Philippe seemed genuinely surprised.

"You're really gonna buy me a new car?" he asked.

"I'm really gonna buy you a new *Porsche*!" I answered.

Philippe said, "If you buy me a new Porsche, then you got a deal." And we shook hands.

The next day I did indeed take him to my favorite Porsche dealer. But what Philippe didn't know was that I had reached out to Evan, my guy at the dealership, beforehand.

"Evan," I said, "I'm coming by tomorrow to buy a Porsche for my new chef. How many cars have I bought from you over the years?"

"Between five and ten," Evan said.

"Yeah, between five and ten," I answered. "And if you ever want to see me again, you're going to take every GT, every Turbo, and all that high-end stuff out of the showroom before we get there. I want my friend to have his choice of any new Porsche Cayenne he wants!"

A Cayenne was, of course, the least expensive kind of Porsche.

Everything went to plan. Evan helped Philippe pick out a brand-new Porsche Cayenne. I brought the paperwork for our new restaurant together, and he signed it right there at the dealership.

And just like that, my new enterprise had been created.

So now I have the best American Chinese food chef in the United States as my partner and have a lease on a space. In addition, my then-fiancée was designing the interior of the space. It looked amazing!

We called the restaurant Philippe by Philippe Chow.

There are many different variants of the last name "Chow" that get anglicized in different ways when people from China come to the United States. There's Chau, Chou, Zhou, and so on. But Chow is the dominant Westernized version.

When I met Philippe, I'd had no idea his last name was Chow. Even so, it was clear that his name would be a happy accident when it came to our marketing.

Around this time, Mike Reda was still working with me, and I brought him in as a partner on the project. Robert Darby, Philippe's friend and translator, also became a partner. I'd written an email to the partners laying out our prospects. It said: If we do $3 million a year, we'll make money. At $2 million, we would still break even. At $4 million, we're making great money. And $5 million, we're printing cash!

Philippe by Philippe Chow opened during the transit strike of 2005. At first, business was slow . . . but it didn't stay slow for long. Word got out about a new Asian restaurant with a great atmosphere, welcoming hosts, and—most important—the best Chinese food in the City. We hit our first $20,000 Saturday in January. Then in February, we had a $20,000 Monday and a $40,000 Saturday. I realized that we potentially had a $10 million-a-year business on our hands! (Previously, I'd thought $4 million was the realistic high end. The property we were renting had housed seven restaurants over the previous fifteen years, and none of them had ever done more than $2 million a year.)

The place was on fire!

Philippe Chow had come out swinging with his slate of classic Chinese dishes and was knocking it out of the park. He had been working at Mr. Chow—underpaid and underappreciated—for twenty-five years, and I was glad to see him finally getting to have his own slice of the American dream. I was so happy for him.

The numbers continued to be great, and I started to think we might even hit $11 million.

At that time, you will remember, my wife was still at *Vogue* . . . and it just so happened that the Met Ball was in May. The head of events at *Vogue* was a very dear friend of ours, and she gave us all the support *Vogue* had to give—which meant booking the *Vogue* after-party for the Met Ball at Philippe Chow. It was hosted by

> People like to get on board with a winner. And when someone like the head of *Vogue* wants to get onboard, you damn sure let them!

Karl Lagerfeld. Anna Wintour supported the move to Phillipe Chow, too. When Anna would come, there would be a table in the middle of the dining room for her, and there would be celebrities and captains of industry all around. Stephanie Winston Wolkoff had been a big advocate of moving the party to Philippe. She got Anna to do a walk-through when we opened Philippe, and then Anna wanted to support us in any way she could.

One funny story about the Met Ball . . .

I got to go in 2008, and my wife was seated at a table with Mick Jagger, Bono, and David Bowie—my literal heroes! I'm drooling. I want to be seated with them. And who do I get seated next to? Some fifteen-year-old girl. (The seating at the Met Ball always split up couples and sat them with strangers of the opposite sex.) When my wife looked over at me and smiled, I surreptitiously gave her the middle finger as I scratched the side of my face.

So I tried to chat with the girl. She said she was a musician and her first record was about to come out. I feigned interest.

But it turned out it was Taylor Swift!

* * *

During this period, I often met people who were not yet prominent, but one day would be. For example, one night at Philippe Chow, a waitress came to me and said that an unruly customer had physically pushed her. I pressed for more details, and she said the whole table was drunk and upset that she refused to serve them more alcohol.

So I went up to this table of two men and two women and said, "Folks, it's time to leave."

The guy who was the leader of the group said, "We're not going anywhere. We're here to have dinner. Fuck you and fuck that waitress. Bring us a new server."

So I did indeed call over a new server. Then I told that server to help me pick up the table. We picked up their table and took it out of the dining room. The unruly group was left sitting there, in the middle of the dining room, in four chairs with no table. It was crowded that night, and everyone was watching this happen.

The leader guy got up from his chair. He's angry, and trying to figure out what to do.

"Now it's time to go," I told them again.

"Me and you, bro," the guy says to me. "You're fucking with the wrong guy."

He leans in and gets nose-to-nose with me.

Then, I suddenly feel a large person grab my shoulder and push me aside. In the same moment, a voice says: "Yeah? You fuck with him, you fuck with me, too!"

The unruly customer immediately stood down and left.

It turned out that this big guy helping me out was Michael Cohen, the lawyer for Donald Trump who would later achieve such notoriety.

I had never met him before, but we became close friends after that!

* * *

Philippe was becoming an important place in the city. Obama even held the meeting to organize the New York arm of his presidential campaign at Philippe.

Believe it or not, when I first got the call that someone running for president wanted to reserve a space, and his name was "Barack Hussein Obama," I thought to myself, "With that name, he'll never win, no matter how patriotic he is. That's like Mr. Mussolini Hitler running against Roosevelt!" But we did the first meeting there, and it was Reverend Al Sharpton, David Patterson, Brian Mathis (Obama's roommate at Columbia), and many others. They asked me if I wanted to meet Obama, and I said sure. I was really impressed. He's one of those people who can just change a room. Later, someone asked me what the meeting was like, and I said: "I think this guy could win. I'm just not sure the Midwest and the South will go for his name."

Of course, he won, and in later years Michelle Obama would become close with Anna Wintour and my wife. Philippe would cater private dinners for Michelle at Anna's Sullivan Street townhouse. (These dinners were my Christmas present to Anna. She was the influencer of influencers . . . before there were influencers. She was the most powerful woman in fashion.)

* * *

In 2006, my daughter Beatriz was born, and in 2008, my daughter Isabel was born. Also in 2008, Philippe was ranked the #1 restaurant in America in terms of sales by square foot. Philippe Chow himself—counting his base salary and his 10 percent—had gone from making $75,000 a year working at Mr. Chow to over $600,000 a year working with me. He was earning what he truly deserved, and I was so, so happy for him.

Now as you might imagine, Michael Chow, the owner and founder of Mr. Chow, was not pleased by any of this. He had initially underestimated how successful Philippe would be. Michael Chow had a reputation for being quick with lawsuits, but it was nine months after Philippe opened before he finally got around to threatening litigation against us. (Believe it or not, I later learned it was Brian the GM who was urging Michael Chow to file the lawsuit . . . and Brian had been responsible for Philippe being created in the first place!) But by the time Michael Chow got his lawyers in the game, the ball was already rolling.

At Philippe, we had the fashion crowd and the rockers immediately. Pretty soon, we had hip-hop, too. One night, Jay-Z came in with Magic Johnson and Kobe Bryant. (A weird detail I remember from that evening is Kobe trying to teach me some Italian. Who knew he spoke Italian?) We were playing Grateful Dead music that night for whatever reason, and it was clear Jay-Z loved the vibe. On his way out of the restaurant, he told me, "I love this place, and I'm going to be a big supporter. I'm gonna do something really cool. Just be patient."

I said, "I don't know exactly what you mean, but your support means the world to me."

True to his word, several months later, Jay-Z and Fabolous come out with a song where he brags about having a reservation at Philippe.

That was the final component! Now we had hip-hop, rockers, fashion, influencers, and socialites!

Soon, we had a regular celebrity poker game in the back where Jerome Bettis and members of the Knicks and Lakers would regularly play.

Oscar De La Hoya held private parties at Philippe, but all I can tell you is that the details would not be suitable for this book!

And when I was on my honeymoon in Mykonos, I suddenly started getting calls from the press saying they were willing to pay me $1 million for "the tape." All I could say was "What tape?" It turned out that a hip-hop mogul and a Hollywood starlet had had sex on a table in a private room at Philippe. The reporters had learned that this room had a security camera. (I called my staff and had them take a look, and sure enough it was there. A million bucks is a lot of money, but I told my staff to delete the video and wipe the server; you build a business by protecting VIPs and celebrities, not by betraying them!)

Everybody started coming to Philippe instead of Mr. Chow, and Mr. Chow went from $8 million a year to $2 million.

Little did Michael Chow know that *all of this happened simply because his manager had disrespected me when I asked to see a menu*! I had had no plans to make my next restaurant high-end Chinese.

The ball just kept on rolling. With other artists taking the cue from Jay-Z, Philippe got mentioned in about thirty other hip-hop songs. So many rappers were now mentioning us, it started to become ridiculous. One lyric went, "I used to eat fried rice, but now I Philippe." Our name had become a verb!

Reservations went to six months in advance. Magic had happened!

We felt like: "What could possibly go wrong? Everything's great. We've done it!"

* * *

Around this time, a powerful developer named Michael Achenbaum came to me and said he was going to be opening the Gansevoort Hotel in Miami in 2007 and he thought the hotel should have its own Philippe as the flagship restaurant. He showed me the plans. It looked wonderful, but I immediately saw that the whole project depended on him successfully renovating a dilapidated hotel called the Rony Plaza into the fancy new Gansevoort. Their partners on this conversion were the Chetrit family, so I went and met with them as well as Michael Achenbaum. It seemed like a good deal.

We got to the lease, and then they suddenly asked me to put up a $2 million construction bond.

I said, "Why am I putting up a $2 million bond when I don't have a guarantee that you're going to finish the renovation?"

Everybody at the table laughed at me, including my own lawyer. They were like: "Stratis, this is the Chetrit family. This is the Achenbaums. They finish things. They're billionaire real estate developers. What's your problem?" And they laughed me out of the table.

> When everyone at the table is laughing at you, that's the moment you know you need to stand up for yourself! No one else is going to.

My partners were worried I was going to kill the deal. Even so, I thought my hesitation was reasonable. How did we know they were going to finish construction? We're gonna have to raise $2 million for this restaurant, but what good is the restaurant if this place is boarded up?

It was the first time in my life I'd been pressured into anything like this, but pressured I was. And I signed on. It was a big mistake!

The Philippe Chow construction in Miami moved forward. It was going to be about 12,000 square feet. The plans for the interior and the build-out looked just beautiful.

Then, of course, things started to go wrong . . .

The first thing that happened was I found out the Chetrits and Achenbaums had gone to war with each other. It was a complicated situation with details I won't go into here, but the upshot was that the Achenbaums bought out the Chetrits. (The Chetrits were masters at knowing when to fold and when to hold. And this one was played poker perfect. Now the Achenbaums owned the Gansevoort outright.)

So they finished the hotel, but it ended up being a far cry from the beautiful diagrams I was shown originally. They "fixed up" the old hotel into a new one in the same way you'd put a Band-Aid on a serious wound! The effect was only cosmetic, and even the cosmetics weren't that good. (The detail that always stuck out for me was that they put a giant fish tank in the lobby of the new hotel, but they could never be bothered to clean it properly. It looked grungy and gross, and they just left it that way.) Almost none of the promised $150 million improvements were made. It was the same ugly windows and the same dilapidated walls of the old hotel. It seemed like the only substantial thing they'd done was to change out some of the furniture in the lobby and replace more furniture in the rooms.

Despite these concerns, we opened the restaurant in December of 2007. Right away, we were killing it. We were doing 1,000 dinners a day, and we were on track to do $13 million in sales for the year. I thought to myself, "Maybe it doesn't matter that the hotel is terrible."

Then the 2008 crash happened. Right away, we found out that Marathon Bank and Credit Suisse had been the lenders that the Achenbaums used to build the hotel. This duo of lenders started saying that a lot of money was unaccounted for. The hotel's business took a serious dive. Money was not coming in, things were not being paid on time, and the lenders started the foreclosure process.

The Achenbaums, meanwhile, wanted to sell the condos that were part of the hotel in order to pay off the debt they had gone into by buying out the Chetrits. Florida implemented a rule saying that there would be no refinancing, however, if a building did not have at least 50 percent occupancy, which the Gansevoort didn't. Simultaneously around this time, the Achenbaums were crushed by losses from dealings with Bernie Madoff. That's when the foreclosures started.

(During this time, I'd ask Michael Achenbaum—the younger Achenbaum—what was going on, but he always stayed pathologically positive. He'd say, "Stratis, we've made so many great moves here." I'd reply, "What great moves are you talking about? I'm hearing you're about to be foreclosed on!" And he'd say, "Listen, I was the first to bring a modeling agency inside a hotel!" Believe it or not, this guy's claim to fame was that he had given the Wilhelmina Modeling Agency a rent-free office inside our hotel—and he seriously thought that that was going to create a buzz and turn things around for us! He really thought this was going to save the property. I looked at him and thought to myself: "Boy, some people are really in the Lucky Sperm Club.")

Luckily, the foreclosure process takes a while, and our Philippe location was still doing great. The week of the Super Bowl in 2009, for example, we did $1.7 million in sales, just for that week! We would sometimes do $250,000 in a single day. We were still killing it. But at the same time, we had to figure out what we were going to do with the threat of the hotel being foreclosed on. It was always creeping closer and closer in the back of our minds. From day to day, we didn't know if the bank was going to swoop in and take over the hotel, and what that would mean for us. Meanwhile, we had a business we were trying to protect that was still doing $13 million a year.

The hotel died gradually, and we could only look on in horror as it did.

First, parts of the hotel started getting boarded up. We'd come into work and see boards on some of the windows and doors. Then the air conditioning went out in most of the buildings. Then one day we came to work and discovered there was no more valet parking service.

All this hurt the trajectory of our sales. Soon we were on pace to do $6 million a year instead of $13 million.

At the same time, we learned that a new W Hotel was about to have its grand opening right beside us.

And can you guess who the flagship hotel restaurant was?

That's right: Mr. Chow.

There was going to be a Mr. Chow literally thirty feet from our building.

> The impulse to get revenge will often prompt people to act irrationally. When these people are your enemies, you can use that to your advantage.

I understood that this was not a coincidence. Michael Chow was attempting to enact revenge.

In retrospect, I should have seen something like this coming. At the time, my wife ran in some of the same circles as Grace Coddington, the former model and creative director at *Vogue* who was married to Michael Chow. Apparently, she would often talk about how furious Michael had become at Philippe Chow leaving. Grace had tried to convince her ex-husband to let bygones be bygones, and to make room for the next generation of Asian restaurants, but this just made Michael Chow even more furious.

The week before the grand opening of the Miami Mr. Chow location in 2009, Michael Chow sent me a lawsuit. It alleged everything you might imagine: I stole his chef; I stole his recipes; I stole his brand identity; I committed corporate espionage; and so on. Michael Chow wanted $44 million in damages.

The suit was meritless, and I could see that a mile away. A judge should have thrown it out immediately on summary judgment.

I hired Anthony Acetta and Vincent Ancona as my lawyers. Michael Chow sent me fifty-six pretrial motions. A typical court case doesn't involve more than five or six. *None* of these motions had any weight or truth value, but I had to answer every one of them. Every answer would cost me between $30–40 thousand in legal fees, and Michael Chow knew it.

Philippe in Miami was, at this point, making less and less money every week, just scraping by. Philippe in New York was still making money, but all of the profit was going to our legal fees.

Around the same time, we also got hit with a labor lawsuit for $2 million. A young lawyer named Maimon Kirschenbaum had created a racket for himself by suing restaurants for violations of tipping and hourly wage rules. In my opinion, almost all of his suits are pettifogging and nitpicking, and he operates on quantity not quality. In the four years before he sued us, he sued about four hundred restaurants, and not one case went to trial.

What Kirschenbaum does is get people who no longer work for you to go in together and file a class action lawsuit alleging that you treated them unfairly.

In my case, he had assembled a group of former Philippe employees who were ready to do precisely this.

Kirschenbaum seems to give these former employees the idea that if they simply sign on to the lawsuit, he can practically guarantee them $20–$30,000 apiece. I think most of them figure, "I'm not an employee anymore, so why not go for the easy money?"

Here's how and why I had become fodder for Kirschenbaum: I had four maître d's working in the front of Philippe in New York, and they would interact closely with all our most prominent guests, like Jay-Z. These guests started naming the maître d's that they wanted to deal with during their visits. They'd call and say: "I want Aris" or "I want Timmy" or "I want Ike." And these maître d's started getting massive, $2,000 tips from these prominent guests at the end of the night.

If you don't work in restaurants, you might not know how unusual that is.

To deal with it, and try to keep things equitable and fair, I called a meeting with my staff. I said, "Timmy's gonna walk out of here with a $2,000 tip from Jay-Z tonight. Do you want that in the tip pool, or do we give all of that to Timmy? He's technically not a server, and he does have some management duties like putting a key in a door to lock up at the end of the night."

At the time, my staff insisted that the tip should go into the tip pool.

Little did I know that the fact that my maître d's locked up at the end of the night meant that, in the eyes of the law, they were managers. Which meant they could not be a part of the tip pool.

By giving my staff the choice to place that tip in the tip pool, I was breaking a rule. Under the law, the tip should have all gone to the maître d', and then he could have chosen to share it with the other employees, if he'd so wished.

I realized I would probably lose against Kirschenbaum if I went to trial, even though what I'd done was meant to create the fairest outcome for the most people, so I knew I would have to play ball. I ended up settling for $1 million with Kirschenbaum and my former staff.

In the meantime, the suit from Michael Chow was ongoing. It's my *very* educated guess that Michael brought his suit against me in Florida and timed it to coincide with the opening of his restaurant right next to mine because he thought it would be good marketing. Michael knew the story of the suit would be in the papers, and he thought he could use it to paint me as the villain who had stolen from him and impersonated his business plan. Meanwhile, he would be painted as "the real deal."

But there are only two states where if you sue someone and lose, you pay *their* legal fees: Florida and Texas. It would have been much safer for Michael Chow to have brought frivolous lawsuits against me in New York. Maybe he had forgotten this, or maybe he was just blinded by rage that I'd had the audacity to compete against him and to offer the same genre of food but with good service and less snootiness. Whatever the reason, the fact that he had chosen to sue me in Florida was certainly foremost on *my* mind!

We finally went to trial in 2011. Michael Chow hired Bert Fields as his lawyer for the case. Fields was a huge and intimidating figure who had represented big names like Michael Jackson, the Church of Scientology, and Bob and Harvey Weinstein.

Fields was so famous that the legal community wrote about any case he took, and they quickly labeled this one "Harvard versus St. John's." Fields was an Ivy League guy, and my attorneys had gone to St. John's in Queens. Personally, I called my lawyers Anthony and Vincent "my two Cousin Vinnys." They certainly had the accents and the look!

The trial started with jury selection. We ended up with a jury composed of mostly younger people, mostly people of color, and many immigrants. All were working class.

The trial got underway, and we tried to make clear that the crux of Michael Chow's argument was that he was claiming to own things that were already public, like the recipe for Peking duck and chicken satay. Our position was not only did he not own these things, but they had been public for centuries.

Still, when Michael Chow discussed these recipes he claimed we had stolen when we hired Philippe Chow, he made the judge clear the audience from the courtroom. It was Michael Chow's position that we were now discussing "trade secrets."

For example, the ingredients to Peking duck are vinegar, honey, salt, pepper, and Maggi Sauce. We would have to take the time to clear the whole courtroom just for Michael Chow to say those five words!

As it turned out, one of the biggest obstacles for our side was getting Philippe Chow himself to grasp the gravity of what was occurring. Believe it or not, even as we were *literally on trial,* in a suit brought by his former employer, Philippe Chow seemed to be unaware of all that was at stake. Philippe still looked up to Michael as a mentor.

This really came through in his testimony.

On the first day of answering questions on the stand, Philippe kept unnecessarily adding that Michael Chow was "a great guy" and so forth. Philippe was careful always to speak of him very respectfully. My lawyers and I were dumbfounded. Why was he being like this? He's talking like Michael Chow is his buddy. Michael Chow wanted to see him homeless on the streets!

After the first day of his testimony, we took Philippe aside and reexplained what was going on. Michael Chow was a bully. Michael Chow was a tyrant who attacked anyone who did anything that displeased him. And now, Philippe, he's coming after you and trying to take your American Dream away. If Michael Chow wins in this trial, you and your family will have nothing. Being penniless is a real possibility for you. And you won't be able to work as an Asian chef for years afterward.

The gravity of the situation finally seemed to dawn on Philippe. At one point, he said, "Reeeeeally?" as if he could not quite credit it.

Apparently, Philippe had thought the stakes were smaller than they were. And/or that the outcome of the trial was not going to impact him personally. We made it clear that this was *very much* going to impact him. If Michael Chow won, all of us would be destroyed.

The next day, when he got back on the stand, Michael Chow's lawyers started off by asking Philippe to confirm who he was and the spelling of his name, just as a formality.

Apparently, our words the night before had done the trick, because Philippe went crazy.

"Spell my name!?" he shouted. "Why should I spell my name for you!? The man you work for is no good. He wants to take everything from me and from my family. He wants to take my house and my money! *I hate this man!* Shame on you, Michael Chow! Shame on you!"

Philippe was so loud, the judge had to threaten him with contempt if he didn't quiet down and answer only the questions he was asked.

My lawyers and I had a good laugh, but, more important, Philippe now understood what was going on . . . and what it would mean if we lost.

There were other amusing moments in the trial, too. At one point, Michael Chow boasted that Michael Basquiat, Keith Haring, and Andy Warhol were all close friends of his. My lawyer Anthony challenged him: "You want me to believe these celebrity artists are all your character references? If so, then where are they? Why haven't you got statements from them to vouch for your character?!"

Anthony knew the law, but he was not the most worldly guy when it came to art. When he was informed that they were all dead, he merely said: "Okay, next question . . ."

Another interesting moment came when Michael Chow claimed that he had created banquette seating.

Banquette seating involves upholstered benches that are often built into the walls of a room. My lawyer Anthony heard "baguette seating" and started going on and on about bread. Anthony had never heard the term banquette. The whole courtroom erupted into laughter by the time the exchange was done.

I was called to testify in the trial. I think Bert Fields was salivating at the thought of getting to grill me one-on-one. He kept me on the stand for a week. (The trial itself lasted seven weeks, which is very long.) Fields didn't get anywhere with me—there were no "Aha! Gotcha!" moments—but by the last day of testimony I was drained and exhausted from dealing with him.

Our judge in the trial was William M. Hoeveler, who had achieved notoriety as the judge in the trial of Manuel Noriega.

On the last day of my testimony, I blew up at Fields and said, "Look, this whole trial is about your client claiming he owns Peking duck and chicken satay, which he doesn't. Those dishes have been around for a thousand years. My grandfather brought the Greek salad to New York, but do you see me complaining or suing people? In a perfect world, we wouldn't have to have frivolous lawsuits about this stuff!"

Judge Hoeveler stopped me and threatened to hold me in contempt.

I shouted, "Judge, how does it make you feel having to go from trying Manuel Noriega to listening to arguments over who owns fried rice? How did you go from Noriega to fried rice?"

The judge ordered me put into handcuffs! My lawyers pleaded for the judge not to throw me in jail. Judge Hoeveler cautioned me that with one more outburst, I would indeed get a week in jail. I shut my mouth from that point on, but I felt as though I had gotten my point across: this lawsuit was ridiculous and was wasting the time of an important courtroom.

Despite my outburst, I thought the case was going well for us. My lawyers had pointed out that Michael Chow had no patents or trademarks on any of the dishes he claimed to own. Further, they had shown that Philippe Chow did not have a non-compete agreement with Michael Chow.

Michael Chow's legal team tried to make the case that his restaurant had become a kind of cultural institution and that I had, in some sense, stolen this institution when I opened a restaurant with Philippe Chow. Michael Chow's team played the court a video featuring celebrities like Warren Beatty, Annette Bening, Robert Di Niro, Jack Nicholson, and Martin Scorsese partying at Mr. Chow. (Much of it was filmed during a birthday party for Michael Chow in the 1970s at which these celebrities had given him shout-outs to the camera.)

But this move set us up to respond by playing some of the thirty hip-hop songs that featured Philippe. And you've got to remember who the jury was: younger people of color with working class employment. By the time we got to the fifth or sixth track, some of the jurors stood up and started to literally dance in the jury box! The point was clear: there was no confusing the world of Jack Nicholson in the 1970s with the world of Jay-Z today.

To drive things home, we also showed the jury a recent photo of Robert Di Niro leaving Philippe. We asked, "Do you honestly think Mr. Di Niro was *confused* about which restaurant he was going to that night?"

The jury came back and found me not guilty of every count except for one, and it was a very minor count. (There had been twelve counts total.) When we had launched Philippe, I had bought online search engine keywords for it, just as I had for FultonStreet.com. I'd bought thousands of keywords. Things like: "Chinese food" and "Peking Duck" and so on. Well, among these, I had bought "Chow" because my chef's last name was Chow! However, this did mean that when people searched for Mr. Chow, Philippe would also come up in the advertised links. There's nothing illegal about doing this, but I think the jury didn't really understand what keyword advertising was or how it worked. Accordingly, they found that this made me guilty of "false advertising."

> **When your enemy is making a mistake . . . let him make it!**

Immediately, I leaned over and asked my lawyer, "What does this single count mean in terms of my legal fees?"

He replied, "Nothing. This is clearly just the jury trying to throw Michael Chow a bone, which they're not supposed to do, and we'll get that reversed on appeal. But even if it stuck, because you were found not guilty on most of the counts, Michael Chow will still have to pay most of your legal fees."

I asked my lawyers, "What are you guys owed right now?"

They said, "About three and a half million."

I ripped a piece of paper from my legal pad and wrote, "Due immediately, $3,500,000." Then I walked over to the opposition's table—where they were still shaking their heads with "How could we lose this?" expressions—and dropped it on the desk in front of Michael Chow.

"Make sure you pay that in thirty days," I told them and walked away.

As I strode out of the courtroom, I overheard Michael Chow say to Bert, "What's this? What's he talking about?"

And I heard Bert reply, "Maybe you weren't listening when I explained it to you, but in the state of Florida, when you sue someone and lose . . ."

And I knew that Bert had already charged him about $10 million. I think Michael Chow thought this trial would be worth it if it put me out of business forever. And yet it had given him nothing but heartache.

In the end, it took until 2014, but Michael Chow finally paid *all* of my lawyers' fees. (You better believe that I've brought up the fact that we need a system like Florida's in New York—to Bloomberg, Giuliani, and everyone in power I could get to listen. Sadly, my words have always fallen on deaf ears.)

* * *

A final interesting note from around this time is that when we did the deal for Philippe Chow in Miami, we were also approached by Bruce Eichner, a prominent real estate developer who was building the Cosmopolitan in Las Vegas. He had borrowed hundreds of millions of dollars from Deutsche Bank to do it.

Eichner wanted us to open a Philippe Chow nightclub in the Cosmopolitan. It was going to be called The Grand Philippe (a name I still think is awesome!), and we would run it. The project stopped when the crash happened. But at that point, I had given Eichner a $250,000 deposit for the rights to the space.

In 2008, I got a letter from one of the guys at Deutsche Bank informing me that Eichner had filed bankruptcy, and that my deposit will have to go through the trustees.

I called Deutsche Bank immediately and said, "You're not stealing my $250,000! My deposit was in escrow, so it's protected against bankruptcy."

Deutsche Bank was intractable. They told me I wasn't getting my money back and I could fight them in court if I wanted.

I said, "*Really* . . . I'm gonna call you back in an hour," and hung up.

An hour later I called back and got the same gentleman at Deutsche Bank.

"Hi, this is Stratis Morfogen again," I said. "Also on the line is a reporter for the *New York Post*."

There *was* someone else on the line . . . but it wasn't a *Post* reporter. It was a cousin of mine.

"I just want this reporter to understand the situation, so he gets it correct in his article tomorrow," I continued. "You've just asked taxpayers to bail your bank out for $2 billion because of bad loans you made during the mortgage crisis, but you also need this $250,000 from me, a small entrepreneur. Have we got that correct? And just so you know, this is for a larger story he's doing on corruption in the banking industry and the use of taxpayer money for bailouts."

"Can I have a comment?" my cousin chimed in. "Also, your name and job title. This story needs to go live tomorrow."

I could tell the Deutsche Bank representative was flummoxed. He hemmed and hawed and said perhaps I misheard him in our earlier call. He was not, he claimed, telling me that I would not get my money back. There were just several factors in play that had to be dealt with.

Anyhow, the next morning I got the wire from Deutsche Bank for the full $250,000!

To this day, I have no idea if I would have won if I'd taken them to court over it. However, I *did* know that to an entity the size of Deutsche Bank, a quarter million was a small price to pay to prevent bad press during the mortgage crisis.

I may not be as rich as Deutsche Bank, but I know how to use the press.

TAKEAWAYS FOR FUTURE DISRUPTORS

- **Another entrepreneur's oversight can be your opportunity for successful disruption.**
- **Trust your gut, even when everyone at the table is laughing at you.**
- **When your enemy is making a mistake . . . don't interrupt him (except to make him even madder)!**

CHAPTER TEN

Neglecting the Small Details Can Utterly Destroy You

American fortunes rise and fall. Each year, approximately 25 percent of Americans make less than they earned in the year prior. (Sometimes it's just a little bit less, but sometimes it's a lot.) Ambitious people like to spend their time focusing on how they can rise. They want to know how to make money and achieve success. This is a wonderful, useful focus to have . . . but it means nothing if you don't protect what you build. Each year, a quarter of us see our fortunes change for the worse. In this chapter, I hope to give a vivid real-world example of how that happened to me. It's an experience that I hope nobody reading this book ever has to go through. It was beset by enemies on all sides—in most cases, by enemies I'd thought were friends—and I learned that those I'd trusted to ensure that my fortune was protected had left a gaping hole in my armor where I could be fatally wounded. If you get one takeaway from this chapter, I hope it's that you understand which small but important details must never be neglected. The only person you can ever trust to handle all the important details to your satisfaction . . . is you.

Despite winning our lawsuit with Michael Chow, the Philippe restaurant in Miami still sputtered and failed. The closing of the hotel was just too much for it to overcome.

Back in New York, I continued to receive strong support from the celebrity community, and from *Vogue* and the Met Ball. The network of restaurants that my partners and I owned during this time was still doing generally okay.

I thought: things could be better, but they could also be worse.

Suddenly, out of nowhere, my partner Mike Reda came to me and disclosed that he had a brain tumor. I, of course, took it on faith. You don't ask to see somebody's medical records when they tell you something like that!

> **Major life events—even in other people's lives—can often portend professional change. Keep your radar up when a business partner tells you they are going through a transition.**

At the same time, Mike Reda also started fighting with Robert Darby. The two could never agree on anything. Soon, they both said they wanted to be bought out of the partnership in Philippe and the other restaurants we owned.

I had recently become friends with the head of a well-known financial services company, a man named Mark Singer, as he was foreclosing on the Gansevoort in Miami. Mark Singer introduced me to another Mark, Mark Grant, heir to a cosmetics retailer fortune, who likewise became a friend. Collectively, these guys were worth about a billion dollars. Mark Grant was dying to have a social life, and I had the sense that he wanted to go into business with me because he wanted to meet celebrities and cool people.

Mark and Mark both said they liked me and wanted to go into business with me. One way they could do that would be to buy out Mike Reda and Robert Darby. It would be a kind of a swap. Mike and Robert out; Mark and Mark in to replace them.

When this arrangement got floated, I said to Mark and Mark: "Wait a second. If this is happening, then I want to be bought out, too. I don't want to be a minority share owner in my own restaurant."

But Mark and Mark flattered me. They said they needed me to continue to grow Philippe. They told me how great I'd been during the trial, and said they needed my business acumen and industry knowledge.

And from the other end, Mike Reda was asking me not to fight this. "Please," he told me, "I don't know how much time I have left."

So I gave in.

I had been referred to my lawyer for the buyout by a friend. My regular guys, Anthony and Vincent, who had helped me during the trial, had dealings with other parties involved and would have had a conflict of interest. So I decided to go with the recommendation on gut. In

> **Never sign documents that leave you unprotected (even if someone says they are dying of brain cancer).**

my opinion, that was the first major step that resulted in my downfall.

I signed papers that would allow the buyout to proceed. Mike and Robert were being bought out, so I was the only one with any exposure. That is to say, I was the only owner remaining who could be held liable for things like debts. What I should have gotten at the signing were indemnifications. The fact that my lawyer didn't do this left me a sitting duck.

So Robert Darby got bought out and walked away with about $4.5 million. I helped make it happen and moved everything along on the back end to make sure he got his money in a timely fashion.

Just to show you what a jerk Robert Darby is, the day he got bought out he told me he was going to give me a gift of $100,000 for helping walk him through the process. I thought, "Well, that'll be a nice envelope."

In addition, Robert Darby decided to go celebrate at a little Italian restaurant I also owned at the time called Ciano. I told him, "Robert, I'm so sorry, but I can't be there tonight to celebrate with you personally. Just leave the check with the manager and he'll leave it for me in the safe." Robert said that would be fine. I also paid for Robert Darby's dinner that night and made sure he got a great bottle of wine. It all cost me $1,000, but I figured, hey, it's the least I can do if I'm getting a $100,000 check. The next day I get to the restaurant, and there's no check. He never left it. Ate my food. Drank my wine. And left *nothing*. It was one final kick in the ass. In my opinion, Darby remains one of the sleaziest guys out there!

> **Envelopes containing a hundred grand are the best kind of envelopes.**

So Robert Darby and Mike Reda get paid out and depart.

Then one year later, Mark Singer starts saying he wants to shut down the restaurants. Suddenly the cash distributions to partners stopped. We had about $1 million just sitting in a bank account, which restaurants never do.

Their motivation is a mystery, but I immediately realized that these are signs that Mark and Mark are trying to strangle me financially. They wanted something, and whatever it is, they wanted to ensure I don't have money to lawyer up and fight it.

And meanwhile, they started to close restaurants.

I couldn't fathom this. What was going on? All of our restaurants were doing at least okay. Why were Mark and Mark closing them?

Then the insult came.

Mark and Mark came to me and offered me $1 million for my shares. I knew my shares were worth about $10 million! Of course, I refused. (Okay, I literally told Mark Singer to stick the shares up his ass. Then he said he would fuck me for this. And then I told *him* to take his best fucking shot!)

Anyhow, six months later the method to their madness became clear when I got a letter stating that I had to appear in US Bankruptcy Court because I was being pushed into involuntary bankruptcy. Who even knew that was a thing! But Mark Singer had found a legal way to partner with our old landlords to compel my bankruptcy.

> You can be betrayed by those closest to you, and those who seem moral can suddenly become amoral at the drop of a hat . . . especially if they will get rich by doing so.

Consider this diabolical move: Mark Singer knew that the law held that if a business owes money to three or more creditors, those creditors could come together as one legal entity to force you into bankruptcy in order to get paid.

To get me out of the picture, Singer was willing to use extreme measures. Armed with this knowledge, Mark looked around for three creditors and found them in the form of the landlords to our restaurants.

Singer and the other partners had started shutting down restaurants in our portfolio in such a way that the landlords of the spaces were left owed money. Mark and Mark did this because they knew that buried in the contracts was the fact that I had the personal guarantee (PG) on all of them, and they didn't. This meant that, eventually, the legal system would realize that I was the one holding the bag. (As I said earlier, my incompetent lawyer should have removed or indemnified me from them when Mike Reda and Robert Darby were being bought out, but he didn't.)

Looking back now, I should have been more suspicious of Singer. His father had been involved with convicted fraudster Michael Milken. Singer had literally been born into a world of corruption . . . into a world where using other people and then stabbing them in the back was normal.

(During this time, Marc Bell had also been an investor in many of the restaurants that were being compelled to close. When I told him what was going on, he sued Singer and Grant. I cooperated to try and help, and the suit was eventually settled. However, Marc still lost a lot of money. This episode made it clear to me that this was a scorched-earth tactic: Mark and Mark were willing to hurt anybody in order to get paid.)

To make a long story short, I lost everything due to this legal maneuvering. Mark and Mark bought my shares for $200,000 from the trustee.

It was doubly painful because Philippe Chow and I had made a personal pact to always support each other in business dealings . . . because we knew we were swimming with sharks.

> **An enemy may turn other partners against you simply by misleading them.**

But I later learned the Marks had essentially given Philippe Chow $100,000 to go against me. (To Philippe's credit, when I discussed it with him years later, he said that he thought taking the money merely meant I would be bought out—and paid fairly—for my shares. Philippe had had no idea of their plan to force me into bankruptcy.)

Just like that, I was completely wiped out. Everything I had built was gone. And it had been taken by these horrible, horrible men! (I believe that the Marks had serious mental problems, especially Grant. For example, Grant would often seem not to know the difference between $50,000 and $500,000 when figures were being thrown around in a meeting. Grant was a yes man and was a laughingstock in social circles. He had a silly little lapdog and a disgusting girlfriend who was always drunk!)

In my opinion, bankruptcy should exist as a shield, not as a sword. Yet Mark and Mark had fashioned it into a sword to get what they wanted from me.

They even tried to go after the homes my wife and I owned. Thank goodness my wife had already put our houses into irrevocable trusts for our children. (She'd done this because of the liquor law liability rules. If someone were to be overserved at one of our restaurants, then drive drunk and kill people, we could be legally exposed personally if a lawyer made a case that it was our policy to overserve. They could go after us personally.) But even though our homes were protected, Mark Singer and his team still tried—unsuccessfully—to use legal maneuvers to go after them. He wanted to put me and my family on the street. He was pathologically angered that I had dared refuse to take his initial offer.

I couldn't believe this group had colluded to steal this thing that I had created and built for years and years. It literally felt like someone had stolen my child. Like something I loved had been abducted, and I didn't know where it was anymore.

I felt so violated, and also down on myself for not having had the safeguards in place to prevent such a betrayal.

I went to my lawyer and told him, "You dumb motherfucker; I think you're the worst fucking lawyer on the planet. How did you allow me to be exposed like this?"

And, of course, he had no answer. Nobody did.

* * *

By 2014, my life seemed to be careening downhill into nothingness. I was unemployed, had no restaurant, and felt like I had lost everything.

I did a lot of reflecting during this period. I thought about how all my life I'd been surrounded by gangsters. Literal, actual gangsters. And yet I'd tried to "move on from all that," you might say, and get in league with a better class of people who were supposed to be more upstanding and respectable. And yet it was these Wall Street, MBA, white-collar types who had revealed themselves to be the true thugs and betrayers.

> Work with enough Wall Street types, and you may find yourself wishing you had straight-shooting, fair-dealing mafiosos as your partners instead.

The gangsters had never done anything like this; they had always been honorable and honest in their dealings with me.

In my opinion, Singer and Grant acted in ways that ought to have been illegal.

For example, I saw Singer and Grant forge State Liquor Authority documents because they could not be on a liquor license; they owned a tequila company, and if you own a company that makes alcohol, you can't have a license to sell at retail other than in a tasting room. So they signed my name.

I brought evidence of this to the SLA, but nothing happened. (At one point, the Marks had tried to sell our restaurants to another company, and the chair of the SLA had called me to ask if I was aware that the company was being sold. Of course, I didn't let that go through.) Yet they had forged my signature—and/or lifted it from an earlier document I had already signed—and Robert Darby's, even though Darby had been bought out three years earlier.

At one point I got a call from Alex Spiro, an assistant DA. I wouldn't have described him as a friend of mine, just a guy who comes to my restaurants and knows me. We weren't close, but I never had any beef with him. Anyhow, he came to me and said, "I'm here because I want you to know what Mark Singer tried to do."

"What could he try to do that he already hasn't tried?" I answered.

"He asked me to fabricate impropriety and fraud on your part—which he knew would be untrue—that could be used to put you in jail," Spiro said. "I told him, 'I've looked at this guy, and there's nothing there. And truth be told, I don't know if you want to go that route, because I hear you've got some SLA issues yourself.'"

Spiro just thought I should know who I was dealing with.

I thanked him, but I was flabbergasted. It was a new low. Singer had gone as far as to ask a DA that I be put in prison on trumped-up charges, just to get me out of the way.

In my opinion, Mark Singer and Mark Grant should have been in jail for their SLA shenanigans. But in the end, they only got a two-week suspension.

It went to trial, but despite their culpability, the judge said he had to be merciful because hundreds of working people would lose their jobs if these men were put out of business. The judge said he was trying to think of the impact on the little guy.

This lack of teeth at the SLA gave Mark and Mark the power to steal my company. I asked the SLA, "If we'd been a little bodega on the corner pulling this shit, but we only had a couple of employees, would you have shut us down?" They answered sadly, yes. The mitigating factor was preserving the income of the workers, no matter how illegal the actions of the owners had been.

What the SLA also wasn't saying out loud was that tax revenue would also be lost if they were shut down. Lots and lots of tax revenue.

It was all about money; it wasn't about the law.

* * *

So everything had been taken from me, and it was clear that the conventional channels were not going to give me justice. I went into a deep depression. It was a very dark time.

> The enemy of my enemy—especially if he holds my enemy's feet to the fire—is my friend!

I'd gone from making $1–1.5 million per year to being too broke to take my kids out to dinner. I was a restaurateur, and now we ate every meal at the house.

I had spent all my money on legal fees. I didn't know what to do. I had a three-year non-compete, which meant I could not open another Asian restaurant for three years. And at the time, knowing Asian restaurants was all the market value I had.

Simultaneously, the Marks decided they weren't content destroying everything I'd built. They also had to salt the earth. They got together with Merchants Hospitality, headed by Abraham Merchant and Rich Cohn, and evidently made a plan to ensure I could never build a successful enterprise like Philippe again. Once again, it was clear to me that these psychopaths wanted to make it personal.

It came out that they were paying an SEO firm about $10,000 a month to buy every keyword related to me and load it with links so that when my name was searched, it would bring the results of everything negative from my life. Every lawsuit against me, even the ones that had been tossed out as frivolous, appeared onscreen. (I actually was not the subject of about 95 percent of them, but my name had been associated with them in some way, and that was enough to scare people.) My own favorite tool had been used against me. If you searched my name, you saw three pages of lawsuits.

My only consolation was the knowledge that they had done this out of fear. Mark and Mark were so afraid of my getting back into the business that they would spend $120,000 a year to try and stop it . . .

or at least slow me down. They knew that potential investors would Google me, and this was exactly what happened.

> **When someone keeps kicking you after you're already down, it's because they fear you rising back up!**

I was always reaching out to investors to test the waters, and despite my many successes, they were all passing on me. That had never happened before.

So I took a grim assessment of myself.

I had zero value to the market.

I had no money coming in.

I was having to depend on money from my in-laws to get by.

Thank God we'd been able to stop our house from being taken.

Anyone who knows me personally will tell you that I'm generally a happy, positive guy. I'm a jokester. I always have good energy.

But there I was at my darkest moment, being none of these things. I was essentially living on Xanax. I was having horrible thoughts all the time. Waking up every morning was torture. I felt worthless.

My wife would say, "Just go get any kind of job. It'll make you feel better."

Legally, I couldn't get a job that had anything to do with Asian food. So I found restaurant manager positions making $80,000 a year. More than the enormous pay cut, the hard part of stomaching it was that I'd never worked for anybody in my life before. I had always been my own boss. From the age of thirteen on, I had always been other people's boss. At nineteen, I had been a boss and business owner. Now I was in my midforties and taking orders from other people.

I didn't know what to do with my life. I thought maybe my life was over.

Around this time, I did get a call from Richie Romero and Bob Collins, business friends who wanted me to consult on a project that would replace the former Limelight nightclub with a new club and restaurant called Jue Lan. That bumped me up to $100,000 a year. But that venture didn't work out well. There were problems, and I was mistreated. (I won't go into too many details, but there was a corrupt investor named Alex Amano and his girlfriend, Naomi, who made a business out of refusing to pay people what they were contractually owed.) After a while, I left it entirely.

I kept trying to do anything that would make me feel like my feet were back on solid ground, like I was no longer falling through the ether. But it just seemed that no matter what I did, things stayed the same. I had lost the old magic.

A lot of my friends turned their backs on me during this period. When I was no longer the "golden boy," they didn't want anything to do with me. To put it another way, you might say I found out who my true friends were.

Jorge Mejia was one of my friends who stuck around during this time. When I started also having trouble in my marriage, Jorge gave me the keys to his apartment and let me live there for six months. Very few people would have done such a thing.

Sant Chatwal, owner of Dream Hotels, was another who helped me get back on my feet during this time. Sant let me stay at the Night Hotel in Times Square for six months

> **When you're down and people want to help you, let them!**

and didn't let me pay for a thing. (I had put my wife through hell during this time, and we had separated.)

My other savior during this time was Niki Maroulakos, my cousin. She literally gave me a blank check when I needed one.

In 2015, my father's kidneys failed. He had to go on dialysis for the last two years of his life. My last conversation with him was February 4, 2016. It was the day he passed. He was really full of water weight and slipping away.

I told my father how I was going to do a restaurant that would bring back the spirit of Chelsea Chop House. I wasn't sure what I was going to name it, but it was going to continue his legacy. I told him how I felt Chelsea Chop House had unjustly never reached its true potential, but I was going to try to take it there, where it deserved to be.

I said, "I'm gonna take that chophouse you did and lift it to new heights. That's gonna be *your* legacy. I'm gonna take it to places you maybe never dreamed of, and I'm gonna get there with *your* logo and in the font you created in 1956. It might be called 'Chelsea Chop House,' or it might be something else, but 'Chop House' is gonna be in there. I'm gonna find the right partners that you could never find. And it's all gonna be done in the spirit of *you*!"

My father was fading as I spoke these words, but I think he understood me. Tears were rolling down his face.

Then I told him I loved him and said my final words, making clear that he'd been an incredible mentor to me, and, more important, the best dad a son could wish for.

And that was my last exchange with my father. The physicians literally had me pull the plug in the next moment. He had been given all the pain medication he could take, and there was no coming back. Still, my father's heart was very strong. I stood by his side until he passed away.

So many people had robbed my father over the years and he had been so hamstrung by his own family members, he had never quite been able to get his restaurants to go where I knew they could.

Even though I was at my lowest moment—and had recently been robbed myself—I genuinely felt that I would be able to fulfill this promise.

As it turned out, this feeling was 100 percent right.

TAKEAWAYS FOR FUTURE DISRUPTORS

- The devil is in the details. Neglecting the small ones, especially the small ones that leave you vulnerable, can destroy you.

CHAPTER ELEVEN:

Disrupt a Model and Miracles Can Happen

Sometimes the night is darkest right before the dawn. A mule will kick the very hardest right before it dies. I've found that when life hands you a situation where it feels like things have become completely unbearable, it may be a signal that things are about to turn around for you. There are periods in every disruptor's life that are all about taking advantage of every opportunity and moving up the ladder, but there are other periods that are simply about surviving. I've been through periods where I "won" by crafting a business model that used disruption to exceed expectations and earn millions of dollars. I've also been through periods where "winning" was synonymous with "surviving." Just getting through a difficult patch can be an incredible victory. But after you survive, it's time to thrive again. No matter how hard things get, hold on to that part of you that wants to use your ideas to change the world. If you do, things just may go your way when you least expect it!

There's an old saying: "Never give up . . . because it's when you're about to give up that the miracle happens."

For me, that miracle was Robert "Don Pooh" Cummins.

Not long after my father passed, Robert paid me an unexpected visit at my house.

"Hey," he said, "get in the car. I want to show you a restaurant I'm doing in downtown Manhattan. Be a consultant. Show me what I can do with this space! I need the old Stratis back!"

I hadn't talked to Robert in years, and yet he suddenly became my cheerleader.

I had first met Robert back in 2005 when he was a regular customer at Philippe. He'd quickly become a close friend. I always saw him at the restaurants I owned, but since being shut out of the restaurant game, I hadn't seen him at all. It had been years since he'd stopped by to see me.

I was in full depression at that time, and Robert could see it. You can't hide deep depression; it's all over your face. I see photos of myself from back then, and I don't look like me.

Still, Robert did his best to shake me out of it. "C'mon, I need the old Stratis back!" he repeated.

For whatever reason, Robert's words seemed to work when nothing else had. It felt good to be needed.

(Looking back, I'm still struck by how much Robert's words helped me on this night. I had seen professionals and been prescribed Prozac. Nothing had worked . . . but Robert's words did. I needed someone who genuinely cared about me and wasn't there because they were being paid, like a therapist. I don't want to knock shrinks if they worked for other people, but for me what worked was Robert!)

I got into the car with him, and we drove off.

Looking back on it now, it feels like getting up and getting into that car with Robert was a test. The universe was testing me. To be very honest, I think I was on my last week of being here. It was a test to get up and walk to that car and drive away with Robert.

But I guess I passed the test.

I got in the car with Robert, and we went to see this space. At the time it was a Denny's.

We were looking at it, and Robert said to me: "I'm planning on doing a Caribbean restaurant in this space. What do you think?"

And I was honest with him. I told him that what I'd do with such a space would be to launch my ideal version of a Chop House; the thing I'd always wanted to do. The thing I had promised I'd do for my dad.

"A steakhouse?" Robert said, clearly not yet feeling my vibe. "Really? I just don't know why you'd want to do that. It's been done so many times."

I'd been trying to deal with my depression by writing a new business plan for a steakhouse. I was thinking of a place that would please a customer like my wife. She doesn't eat beef . . . so what could a steakhouse have on the menu that would make her excited to come through the door?

"No," I said to Robert. "A steakhouse has never been done the way *I* want to do it, because it's never been done by someone with *my background*—in chophouses, in Greek food, and also in Chinese food. Ask any good Chinese or Chinese American chef, such as my chef Skinny Mei who has been with me for fifteen years, what they think of when they think of a 'chophouse.' They see someone working as a 'chopper,' which is a respected position in a kitchen, but their vision goes far beyond what we see as Westerners. I want to make a chophouse where a pescatarian like my wife could go and still find something to eat. I want to marry dim sum and chops. I want to bring Chinese sensibilities and *possibilities* to an American chophouse. I want to disrupt the whole damn model!"

Then I told Robert about my concept of "LSD," which was a key part of my business plan.

"It'll be salt and pepper and ginger and garlic lobster," I explained. "Dry-aged porterhouse steak. And authentic Peking duck. Lobster, Steak, Duck. LSD. That's *my* version of a chophouse."

There was suddenly a gleam in Robert's eye. We ended up standing there in front of the Denny's and talking for an entire hour about my vision.

The next thing I know, Robert has brought his other partner, David Thomas, in on it.

And I'll give both of them a hell of a lot of credit! They had already started construction on their Caribbean restaurant, but they chose to halt everything to go with my vision. To create. To disrupt. To do a chophouse differently from how it's ever been done over 150 years. To disrupt a menu that hasn't changed for decades or centuries by marrying Beijing Chinese food with an American chophouse.

The Irish brought this culinary wave to us in Brooklyn; that's where the first eleven chophouses in America opened. They were serving mutton chops, lamb chops, pork chops, and so on. And there's nothing wrong with that, but Robert and David understood that it was time to disrupt that model. We were going to do a chophouse but have Peking duck and chicken satay and Kung Pao shrimp. Everything was going to be Asian, except the steak. The steak would stay true to what an American chophouse is, and the Asian dishes would stay true to the Beijing culinary arts.

So we went in as partners to bring this remarkable creation into being.

But we didn't have a name!

I knew that "Chop House" would be part of it, but I wasn't sure about the rest . . .

One day we were trying to think of names, and I was sitting at the window of our new space, looking out at the Brooklyn Bridge.

"Robert," I said to my colleague. "Let's do the bridge. We can call it The Bridge Chop House."

"That sounds pretty good," Robert said. "I actually really like it."

So for a moment we were off and running with that.

But I kept looking out the window.

"Or what about City Hall Chop House?" I said. "City Hall's right there. Or Wall Street Chop House. We're close to Wall Street."

I liked all of these, but none of them had real magic yet.

"Wait a second," I said. "The Brooklyn Bridge is thirty feet away, and Brooklyn is where chophouses were created by the Irish in the 1850s. This could be a tribute to all of that! But . . . there's no fucking way that name's available."

Then I went online, and wouldn't you know . . . it was!

I about ripped my pants pulling my credit card out of my wallet and securing that name. In a flash, BrooklynChopHouse.com was ours! Nobody else had taken the name anywhere. I couldn't believe it. The word "Brooklyn" had gained so much equity in terms of consumer products. Brooklyn has become a very big brand nationally. It's bigger than the word Manhattan. It's bigger than any other borough. And here, somehow, Brooklyn Chop House was available.

Again, I'm not a religious man, but in that moment, it felt like someone was up there watching. How else to explain the synchronicity of everything coming together for us?! It felt *impossible* that the name should be available in this day and age! But we locked it all up, from web domains to social media, to keywords. It was all ours.

* * *

Formulating the menu at Brooklyn Chop House was a really interesting process.

When we got down to the dumplings, I was like, "When you go to a typical chophouse, you can always get a great burger, too. But I don't want to do a burger. I want to do a bacon cheeseburger shumai. I want to do a lamb gyro dumpling. I want to take my grandmother's recipe for a gyro and put it into a dumpling instead of a piece of pita bread. I want to do a Philly cheesesteak dumpling, and a Reuben dumpling. Instead of sauerkraut, we're gonna do bok choi."

We sat down and we wrote the menu out.

When we looked at the finished menu, my partners and I agreed: either this would be a gangbusters success . . . or we were gonna confuse the fuck out of everybody and flop immediately!

* * *

We opened Brooklyn Chop House in October of 2018, and it was a monster success from day one.

The dumplings were a big part of this.

Whereas in most restaurants that serve dumplings you might get one order of dumplings per table, at Brooklyn Chop House, people were coming in and every person at the table was ordering dumplings because people wanted to try all the different kinds! For example, a party of six might come and order the LSD, but then also eight to ten different orders of dumplings. This customer behavior quickly became typical!

And the LSD was so successful that we started hashtagging #LSD on Instagram. Believe it or not, we got a message from the government after the first year saying we were being investigated for the promotion

> When success shows you the way to further success, let it! Chase it wherever it takes you!

of narcotics. Apparently, 3,500 people hashtagged "LSD" in connection to our account. Like we were the Silk Road or something, instead of a restaurant.

I sent the regulators a tweet that was all emojis: A lobster, a steak, a duck, a dumpling, and a middle finger! That was my answer to their investigation.

Sadly, to this day #LSD has been removed from Instagram. It was all because of us! I believe at that point we hit legendary marketing status.

Meanwhile, accolades were pouring in. *Thrillist* named us Best New Restaurant and *Newsweek* called us the best steakhouse in New York.

I soon realized that what we had in Brooklyn Chop House was not just a very successful steakhouse, but a blueprint for our next venture: Brooklyn Dumpling Shop.

By early 2019, Brooklyn Chop House had doubled all of our projections. We were hoping for a $5–6 million restaurant, and we went right to $8 million. (We got to $12 million when things began to open up after the pandemic.)

When we realized that we were seeing one order of dumplings per person, we knew we had to do something with that information. Up to this point, people in the restaurant business would have said such a thing was statistically not possible. It was a million-to-one odds, according to perceived ideas, that you'd be able to sell an order of dumplings per person. It just wasn't thought to be doable in the restaurant industry. We had disrupted that notion quite successfully. But now, the question was what to do with our success.

In the summer of 2019, I said to my partners, "For our next step, we need to disrupt the sandwich shop and the dumpling shop. I want to open something called Brooklyn Dumping Shop. And it's essentially going to serve a two-ounce sandwich."

My partners had never heard of such a thing, but they were on board. They thought it was cool. I told them how I thought it would help us get new kinds of customers.

"Back when I was a little kid working for my dad," I told Robert and Dave, "I'd see people served a pastrami sandwich with meat piled up a foot high, and I'd think, *That looks disgusting!* The sort of thing that Katz's Deli is famous for? That was never for me! But if you gave me that same food, but sized like a cheeseburger, I'd eat it all day. For me, that big sandwich was intimidating. I think lots of younger people—people between five and fifteen, say—are intimidated by certain foods. It's too big, or feels too exotic, or they don't know how to eat it. But I think they'll try it if it's a dumpling. It's not intimidating; it's a small bite. I think that's the way to go for the TikTok generation."

Robert and Dave loved it. In the days that followed, I wrote the business plan for Brooklyn Dumpling Shop.

In the course of doing research, I found out that nine out of ten quick service restaurants that fail do so because of payroll. They run out of money paying employee wages.

> Always do your research! Know an industry before you disrupt it. Learn past outcomes so you can forge different ones in the future!

At the same time, I'm thinking about how when I drive down the LIE to the Midtown Tunnel, there are no more people taking tolls; it's all automated. I don't have to stop and give money to anybody. So I'm thinking to myself, I want to do the same thing with a quick service restaurant. I think the TikTok generation already knows what they want, and they don't particularly enjoy talking to cashiers.

Continuing this research, I looked into the history of the automat.

If you're not aware, automats were restaurants that gained some popularity in the early twentieth century because the food was entirely served by vending machines. It wasn't the kind of food we think of as "vending-machine food" now, but proper dishes, just all inside of vending machines. I thought to myself, while I'm disrupting things, why not disrupt the automat?

I researched the history of the automat—why it had succeeded initially, and then faded away. Automats in New York were launched by a company called Horn & Hardart in 1902. After the Spanish Flu outbreak ended, they opened thirty-six locations. They were up to eighty locations in New York by the 1940s. It was a 100 percent contactless restaurant. At its height, automats in the USA were serving about 800,000 meals a day.

By the 1970s, however, the automats were dying. One reason for this was their annoyingly inferior technology. The automat machines remained coin-fed. There were no credit card processors or dollar bill receivers. You had to physically go get nickels and quarters and put them into the machines. Not so convenient! Technology—or, more accurately, the lack of it—killed the automat in the 1970s. Technology *killed* the automat.

Another reason for the automat's failure was the rise of fast food. People felt like, "Why go to an automat when I can go to a fast-food restaurant and get freshly prepared food almost as quickly, and I can pay with bills or a credit card instead of fiddling with loose change?"

As I went about creating the disrupted, reinvented automat (a.k.a. Brooklyn Dumpling Shop), I wanted to keep everything about automats that had worked and draw on new technology to address the factors that had led to their downfall. We would have fast lines. We would have technology to take payments. We would be able to compete with any other quick service restaurant.

In a world where we have driverless cars, I was confident we would be able to bring the automat back. The consumer will be able to control the whole automat experience through their phones. They can place an order, receive a QR code, schedule a time to pick up their order, and scan their phone when they walk into the store. Then the heated or refrigerated locker will automatically open, and the customer can take their food and go!

To make this happen, I initiated a partnership with Panasonic (with some parts being sourced to another company called Ondo) to create the technology that would be needed for this new version of an automat. The result is a hi-tech automat experience. It's contactless, and your only interaction as a customer is with the locker where you pick up your food.

In September 2019, Panasonic delivered a prototype of how our automat would work, and it was amazing; it worked perfectly. The lockers were heated and refrigerated, and everything worked from a smartphone. Most important, these changes would allow me to reduce 50 percent of my payroll. And, again, payroll costs are the #1 killer in fast casual.

We signed our first lease for four hundred square feet of store space in January of 2020. We were locked in and ready to go. Our location was on the corner of St. Mark's Place and First Avenue. We were off to the races.

Boom! COVID hits.

Here's my funny story about COVID. The week before it hit, I went to my doctor.

> **Change always presents opportunity. Even horrible changes like the ones that came from COVID.**

He said, "Why are you here? You're not due for a checkup."

I said, "I'm here because I've never had all three things in my life working well at the same time. My marriage is good. My kids are happy and healthy. And my business is thriving. So, doc, something else must be wrong. I never have so much good fortune. It's gotta be my health!"

So my doctor checks me out, and when the bloodwork comes back, he says: "Stratis, you're good. There's nothing wrong with you.

You've had enough bad luck in your life, so now you've just got some good luck. Accept that."

Then, the month the COVID shutdown began, I called my doctor and said, "I told you!"

All of a sudden, where I had a $12 million a year restaurant in Brooklyn Chop House, it was now eking by at $1 million. Everything was collapsing.

I had just signed the lease for Brooklyn Dumpling Shop, so I went to the landlord and brought up that they also had an empty store for rent right next to my place. They wanted $9,000 a month for it, the same as what I was paying for my Brooklyn Dumpling Shop location.

I said, "Listen, you're never going to rent that place out during COVID. But I can use it to expand Brooklyn Dumpling Shop and build a beautiful flagship store. To do that, I want two years rent free, and then $2,000 a month after that."

Why was I so brazen? Because I knew what COVID was, and what it was going to do.

They gave me some pushback at first, but I explained how every year, after the year at $2,000, they could increase the rent by another few grand. I also said that if they were game to play ball, I'd take the lease right now. Like, sign the documents *today*.

The landlord knew what was up, and they took that deal.

So I broke down the wall and created the thousand-foot flagship store for Brooklyn Dumpling Shop.

By the end of 2020, Panasonic and Ondo finished delivering the last of the automat equipment. We thought we were going to open at the start of 2021 but kept being slowed by unpredictable shutdowns ordered by the government.

Meanwhile, the automat machines were plugged in and ready to go, and they had these beautiful red and blue lights. People started walking by and just taking pictures of the cool-looking machines and sharing them on social media. It started going viral on Instagram. Everyone was like, "Look at this. Someone's doing a twenty-first-century version of an automat!"

And then the press started coming to call. All of a sudden, we were in twenty magazines within a three-month period.

Then Dan Rowe, the entrepreneur behind Qdoba, Halal Guys, and a bunch of other big players in the fast casual space, came calling. He said, "I know this field, and because of what you've done, how you've designed things, your project is going to be very franchisable."

We met in person and hit it off. Soon thereafter, we signed a contract. Dan's team sold fifty franchise locations of Brooklyn Dumpling Shop before the first store was even open. I've been assured that that has never happened before in the history of franchising! Most of the time, franchises will only begin to sell after proofing out a model for a minimum of two years. And there I was, just waiting for the government to let me open my store to sell my first dumpling, and I was selling franchises. Soon, people were throwing money at me to buy territories in major metro areas. Industry observers and experts were looking at me and scratching their heads.

So, was all the hype correct?

In a word: yes!

We finally opened our first location in May of 2021 to gangbusters success. Lines out the door. People loved the dumplings. Moreover, they loved the customer experience. They loved coming in and opening their food locker with a swipe of their phone. You can see it on their faces;

> **When you generate a positive customer reaction, the first thing a customer will do is post it on social media. The bigger the reaction, the bigger chance of your going viral!**

whenever you make a guest feel smart and delighted, you've won.

The franchise world saw this and came back to take another bite!

Before I knew it, I was up to 165 franchises sold. (By the time this book comes out, my estimate is we'll be at around 310.) Our first franchise opened on 2/22/22 near the University of Connecticut. Every three weeks for the rest of 2022, we'll open a new shop. During 2023, we'll open a new shop every week. And in 2024, that's projected to go to two per week.

How eerie is this: a hundred years ago, Horn & Hardart exploded after the Spanish Flu receded. Now, a hundred years later, I am poised to do the same! It's the same exact thing, to the year.

(As with any successful disruptor, there will always be haters. We were disrupting the dumpling and the sandwich, and actually doing it! Yet we got backlash from some in the culinary community calling our work "cultural appropriation" and "blasphemy." None of these accusers had really researched our business; they didn't know I had two Black partners, one Asian partner/chef, many Asian employees, or anything else. But these sorts of accusations will come whenever you're upsetting the status quo. To me, food brings cultures together. It always does that. That's just a natural law. In my opinion, anyone who is saying otherwise is part of the problem.)

Anyhow, there was one interaction with a customer that really solidified my feeling that we had attained our goal with Brooklyn Dumpling Shop.

This customer came over to talk to me one day at the shop. She was in her sixties, and she started by telling me that the first time she came inside Brooklyn Dumpling Shop, she immediately felt ready to turn around and leave.

"I didn't want to be in a place that made me feel like I needed an MIT degree to order food," she explained. "But your greeter was so kind, and she walked me through all the technology. She showed me how easy it was to order dumplings. So I stayed and ordered. Now I've been back five times in the last six weeks! But I've also been to a

Chipotle and a McDonald's and a Starbucks. And I'll tell you, I can't look at their cashiers the same way anymore. I'm thinking, *Why the hell am I even dealing with a cashier when I could do this myself on my phone?* These people are trying to upsell me on a pumpkin latte, when I already know what I want. You've changed the way I look at them.

"Let me give you an analogy I came up with," she continued. "You know what this is like? It's like me driving through the Midtown Tunnel where they're gonna scan my E-ZPass, but instead there's a toll booth and I gotta put on my brakes and stop and

> **If you're in hospitality, you're in the reaction business. Never forget that! The bigger a customer's reaction, the bigger your success is going to be!**

pay them. After eating at Brooklyn Dumpling Shop, I feel like other restaurants are a toll booth. And another thing. Years ago, when they got rid of the toll booths, I worried about the toll booth workers losing their jobs. But I will tell you now, if they ever were to come back, I'd be furious! Because I didn't know I needed it until I experienced it. And that's how I feel dealing with your restaurant."

I liked this story for a bunch of reasons, but not least because I wasn't the only one who thought of the toll booth example!

Another way that Brooklyn Dumpling Shop is creating disruption is in the way we are setting up franchises. This is a big reason for our success, and important for me to include here.

With most franchises, they give you a manual—or "train-ual"—and some instructions on running the franchise, but then you're basically on your own to figure it out!

Our way is different. When a franchise opens, I go in personally with a team of four and show the franchisee how to do everything from packaging to inventory management, to supply chain, to setting up the technology, down to hanging the sign on the door. We do it all for the franchise owners, and, to me, this explains why our franchise business is blowing up.

The day our Brooklyn Dumpling Shop franchise location at UConn opened, we sold a hundred more franchises. A hundred sold in a single day. This was because potential franchisees saw how seamless it was to open, saw how much support they got, and the enthusiasm for the product. My team and I set the whole shop up in just four days. On that first day at UConn, we expected to have lines down the block and sell three- to four hundred orders of dumplings. We had the lines down the block all right, but we sold a thousand orders of dumplings. (Our franchisee was so pleased that, on that very same day, he upped his own order from ten franchises to forty!) People were waiting online in freezing weather just to get an order of dumplings, and it was all over Instagram. The TikTok generation, which is basically university students, is our demographic, and we know that for sure. (We had doubters and naysayers, but at not quite eight hundred square feet, our store is generating a thousand orders per day. People are lining up thirty minutes before the store opens.)

People asked our franchisee Matt Rusconi:

- How is corporate support?
- How is the Automat tech running?
- What is the food cost?
- What is the payroll cost?
- Would you open another store?
- And finally, is this guy Stratis full of shit, or is he the real deal?

In every case, Matt answers that we are there for him, things are running great, costs are controlled, he wants to do more stores, and I'm for real!

We are disrupting the way franchise deployments have typically been done. We still provide people who buy Brooklyn Dumpling Shop franchises with all the paperwork required by the state; we have that in common with competitors, yes. But everything beyond that is different. We're literally coming in and setting up the restaurant like it's ours, *then* handing it off to the franchisees. (At the time of this writing, my new passion is learning to fly. Not just because it's exhilarating, but because by flying my own airplane I can easily hop between multiple franchise locations in the same day.) To be honest, this disruption *needed* to happen in the world of franchises. Someone needed to come along and do it the right way.

I'm glad we had that chance.

TAKEAWAYS FOR FUTURE DISRUPTORS

- **Right when you're about to give up is when the miracle can happen.**
- **Success brings success—let it!**
- **Know the past to know the future.**

CHAPTER TWELVE:

Giving Back, Investing in Yourself, and Engaging with the Larger World

Nobody exists alone. We need one another. Disruptors need things to disrupt. They also need communities. When disruptors craft a successful business venture, it is usually because they have changed the world to create a product or service that connects with a community of customers in a new way. Once a disruptor has that success, I believe that it is vital to give back to the community that allowed the disruptor to be successful. It is supporters of your business that have given you the opportunity to prosper. It is now important for you to provide opportunities to others.

Being a disruptor means disrupting the old order so that new opportunities can be created for those around you. When one of your business ventures has success, you'll find that you have the newfound means to do this. For example, at Brooklyn Dumpling Shop, our passion for giving back led us to initiate a program for young Black and Brown businesspeople. A lot of franchises talk the talk when it comes to this sort of thing, but we are demonstrating a real commitment from the start.

We decided that we would give a store away every two years to a young Black or Latinx entrepreneur. In the franchise world, things are mostly white. Only about 5 percent of all franchises are sold to Black and Brown entrepreneurs. That's something that needs to change. We all felt that we needed to do something about it.

So in March of 2022, we announced that we're giving away our first Brooklyn Dumpling Shop to a young entrepreneur named Johnny Angel. We selected him out of 1,800 applicants through a program announced on *Good Morning America*. (I appeared on the show

> **Give back to the communities that supported you and do it in a <u>meaningful</u> way!**

and made the announcement.) Johnny will have his own restaurant in Hoboken and be a partner. We also provided him with nine months of free training and mentoring.

Going back even earlier, after opening Brooklyn Chop House, there were signs that the specter of racism in America was something that my industry still needed to deal with.

Both of my two partners in Brooklyn Chop House are Black. And I had worked in the nightclub industry, which always meant a diverse cast of people. A lot of nights at the nightclubs were either official or unofficial nights where people of color would gather to be with one another. I might be one of the only white faces in the room. So I had lots of fans from my previous ventures going into Brooklyn Chop House. (In my experience, if Black culture loves you, they *really* love you!)

When we opened Brooklyn Chop House, I wasn't thinking about the fact that most of the residents in the building above it were white people. This was the Beaux Arts building in Manhattan, which can be very high-end. But it wasn't long until we had complaints from condo associations about too many people outside the restaurant hanging out, congregating, or waiting to be seated.

I think the crucial detail here is that in the early days of Brooklyn Chop House, our customers were about 80 percent people of color. Part of this was because my partners were Black, and part of it was my fans from the nightclubs, and part of it may have just been a random coincidence.

Anyhow, some of the condo association people stayed civil, but others didn't give a fuck and would circulate letters or emails that went full-racist against our customers. These letters would literally use words like "filth" to characterize the people waiting for a table outside. There was a group of five to seven of these tenants who even began building a legal case against us.

When it came to standing my ground when it comes to defending people of color, I look to my friends for mentorship and inspiration.

I've long been friends with Hawk Newsome, the founder of the New York chapter of Black Lives Matter. Do I always agree with *every-thing* he says? No, but I love his spirit, and I admire his tenacity and honesty. I think any aspiring disruptor can learn a lot from his take-no-shit, take-no-prisoners approach to things. I think he is genuinely working to level the playing field. If you want to allow people of every race to have a fair shot, then the ones who haven't been treated fairly are going to have to break some eggs. I think Hawk does outstanding work, and I try to meet up with him for cigars whenever we can find the time!

I didn't know that opening up Brooklyn Chop House would coincide with the Black Lives Matter movement. I couldn't have known the impact of two Black partners in the venture, and of having over two decades of experience catering to Black customers in different capacities. But when it all came together, it sure felt like something cosmic was going on.

All I can say is that I agree with the activists who say that Black opportunity has to be on a level playing field. Black people in America have been fucked for generations. Now that a consciousness of that is finally setting in, it can only be good. Now that people actually want to support Black-owned businesses, I can only do my damnedest to make that happen.

* * *

In addition to handling racists from condo associations, another lesson for me was how to handle Yelpers. This goes under the header of "community engagement" with which every disruptor must learn to deal.

> **Engaging with your community of customers might not be your favorite part of the job, but you have to do it!**

Some customers today try to use Yelp as a form of extortion. It doesn't matter what business you're in; you're going to encounter people who will use bad reviews as a threat. They think the customer is always right, and that any business should grovel for them at their whim.

Now, when my business makes a legitimate mistake, I always go above and beyond to make it right. But I'm not talking about that here. I'm talking about entitled and abusive customers.

For example, one night a woman came into Brooklyn Chop House. She had made a reservation for eight people and said they would arrive at eight in the evening. They showed up an hour late and said they now had twelve people. This was at a juncture when we were booked weeks in advance.

I said to the woman, "I'm sorry, but I can't seat you. You might have to wait a couple of hours."

She said, "If you don't seat us, then every one of us will write you a one-star Yelp review."

I said, "Go ahead. I'll respond to it."

She said, "I'm serious. You have to seat us now."

I replied, "There's the door. Money's not a good enough reason to be threatened. I'd like you to leave."

I look the next day, and there they are: ten one-star reviews on Yelp. Most of them are from accounts with no other reviews, meaning they were newly created just to disrespect us. It's also evident that most of the "reviews" are whole and complete fabrications, such as, "We saw cockroaches running around in the kitchen; there were hairs in our food," and so on. I was like: You weren't anywhere near the kitchen, and you weren't served any food!

It was as brazen as it was false.

So, I responded to the review of the woman with whom I'd spoken directly. It was a public response that anyone could see.

"Look," I said, "you caught me on a bad day. I'd like to buy you all dinner."

She replies, "Really? You were such an asshole yesterday, and now you want to buy us dinner?"

I replied, "Yes, I'd like to buy you dinner. I'm sorry for what happened. Let's start over."

She said, "Okay. What time do you want us?"

I replied, "Let's do this . . .," and I sent her a link from my OpenTable account. The link showed that I'd made her a reservation for a nearby Red Lobster for eight people on the following Saturday.

I added, "I'll buy you dinner, but it's going to be at Red Lobster in Times Square, because that's where you belong!"

And it went viral. Every part of this exchange had been public. People took screenshots, and soon it was being shared all over the world. Talk about free advertising!

I went to Yelp and told them that when a review is questioned, they should require proof that the person actually dined there by having them produce a receipt. Yelp replied that they don't have the manpower to do that. I couldn't believe it. They can put a small business out of business, but they can't check a receipt!

See what I did there? I disrupted. I came at the situation from a new angle. I used the platform in a way that this threatening customer and Yelp itself had not expected!

And just for the record, my businesses always get at least 4.5 stars on Yelp!

* * *

Speaking of social media, when I opened up the first Brooklyn Dumpling Shop location, the grand opening event had three members of the press there to interview me. Someone from the *Wall Street Journal,* someone from the *New York Times,* and someone from *New York* magazine. In the midst of these interviews, my daughter Isabel—thirteen years old at the time—kept calling me. And she'd text, "Dad, pick up." I'd reply that I couldn't talk right now, I was doing important media interviews. I was talking to the *Wall Street Journal.*

She'd reply, "Dad, they don't matter."

Over the phone, I gently tried to explain, "Honey, these people are actually very important to your dad's success and his new business."

"They don't matter," my daughter insisted.

I let her go. She was speaking nonsense!

Later in the day she reached out to me again. This time I told her I was with *New York* magazine and still couldn't talk.

"Dad, I need to speak to you," she said.

But I had to hang up on her. I was doing important things on the day of my big opening!

She kept calling me.

Finally, I picked up again.

"Honey, now I'm with the *New York Times*," I told her. "You gotta give me a few more minutes."

"Dad," she said, "I'm trying to tell you that you've gone viral on TikTok. You've got sixty million views from someone talking about how good your dumpling shop is. That's what matters. Your audience cares about TikTok. That's what counts. Not these newspapers and magazines."

I thanked her for her opinion and hung up the phone.

The day after the opening, we still had lines around the corner to get into the restaurant. It was mostly families with children, students, or groups of kids. I would ask them, "How did you hear about us?"

Invariably, the answer came back, "It was TikTok!"

The lesson I learned from my thirteen-year-old is that the old guard doesn't have a monopoly on influence anymore, and when you're making a product that can be enjoyed by young people (like

> The rising generation may show you new ways of engaging with your community. You'd be a fool not to sit up and take note!

dumplings), what matters is landing in the social media that's going to connect with that generation.

We still meet tourists at Brooklyn Dumpling Shop who've come from overseas. We chat with them, and like many tourists, they share that they have "hit lists" for their visit: seeing a Broadway play, seeing the Statue of Liberty, and so on.

But now, whenever someone in the tourist group is younger, they share that their list includes visiting Brooklyn Dumpling Shop because they saw us on social media. (As of this writing, there's something like 160 million views for Brooklyn Dumpling Shop–related videos just on TikTok alone!)

* * *

Why is Brooklyn Dumpling Shop exploding now? A big part of the answer is because we invested in ourselves and in *building a payroll first*. This is a disruption of the dominant franchise model, and something that many entrepreneurs ought to become familiar with.

We got funded and invested in ourselves, and *then* we started making money.

There's an old saying: "You've got to lose thousands to make millions, and you've got to lose millions to make billions." There's no shortcut to this. It's certainly what we did at Brooklyn Dumpling Shop. We first built a massive payroll. Our payroll was bigger than our sales. But then we grew into our payroll. Building a payroll means investing in people, SOPs (standard operating procedures), TOPs (technological operating procedures), investing in technology, investing in supply chain, investing in distribution. All of this is expensive, especially the supply chain. You've got to do 100 sample runs of product with your supply chain provider.

And what about product development?! We've found that it takes about fifty thousand dumplings to make sure that we've got the taste profile correct. In this stage, it costs us a dollar to make a dumpling. And that's got to be done for every flavor and variety across the whole menu.

* * *

Here's another important story about both Brooklyn Dumpling Shop and Brooklyn Chop House, and how we seek to engage.

Patti LaBelle, who has been a huge friend and supporter, came to Brooklyn Chop House as a customer not long after it opened.

Right off, her son tells me, "Listen, I know you're famous for dumplings here, but my mother hates dumplings. Don't even *try* recommending them."

So, me being me, I sent ten different kinds of dumplings to her table. I sent my pastrami, my Reuben, my bacon cheeseburger, my Philly cheesesteak, my Impossible—a bunch of 'em. I knew these were things Patti would be familiar with as sandwiches, but I wanted her to try them as dumplings.

So Patti tries these dumplings, and she absolutely loves them.

She turns to me and says, "Stratis, I'm taking you to Arkansas!"

And I knew what that meant! She was going to use her relationship with Walmart to pitch my dumplings to the largest retailer in the country.

Just two weeks later, we found ourselves down in Bentonville making our pitch to all the head buyers. Patti's son, Zuri, came along, and so did Charles Suitt and Alex Thompson from Patti's organization. I walked out of that meeting with a 1,000-store purchase order. The only issue was we didn't have any packaging.

Everyone around me at the time said, "Stratis, we've gotta go with a more pastel feel. They want blues and pinks and gentle yellows from their frozen food products. Everything is always soft here."

And I said, "No! That's not the approach. We want to pop in a way that differentiates us from this army of pastel colors. We don't want to join the status quo. We need to come with Brooklyn! We need to come with the color black! Maybe there could be a watermark of the Brooklyn Bridge, too. And when the customers see a packaging looking like *that*, there'll be no mistaking it. We're gonna stand out by the doing the opposite of everybody else. The marketing and eye-attention will be priceless."

We had big arguments about this. I stuck to my guns. I wanted a black package marked with the bridge that looked hip. When we took the idea back to the Walmart buyers, they agreed with me! They were like: "We get it. This could be really cool. It will also help Walmart look hip!"

So that's how we agreed on the packaging. These products are now slated to be in Walmart stores by the end of 2022.

* * *

And here's some more synchronicity: The first Brooklyn Dumpling Shop location in Long Island is going to be on Stewart Ave., right across the street from where I went to school as a kid. It seems like some kind of cosmic justice that I used to be sitting in class, ignoring whatever lesson the teacher was talking about, but looking out the window and imagining owning my own restaurant. And now a restaurant of mine is going to be right where I was looking! And I didn't pick that location; it's just where we landed. I'm not a traditionally religious man, but I do believe there's a higher power involved on that one!

Maybe my father's behind it . . .

One of my favorite commercials has always been the Dunkin' Donuts "Time to make the donuts" commercial, where the guy would get up early in the morning to make his donuts.

Well, with the success of Brooklyn Dumpling Shop in 2021— and its historic place as the only automat in the business right now— we're now embarking on a "Got to make the dumplings!" advertising campaign. I'm disrupting the traditional commercial and giving it a brand-new spin.

Pretty soon, we're going to be known as "the Tesla of automats"!

* * *

Another lesson I learned around this time is that you can think you're done with an industry, but that doesn't mean it's done with you!

As I noted earlier, as a teen I always played in rock bands. I was a drummer and loved playing the drums. This exposure to bands allowed me to draw on my music-industry knowledge when I took over the restaurant at Partyland and grew my first real business.

When I was still in high school, my friends and I were serious about the music thing. We all had jobs as busboys and used the money we made to pay for studio time to cut demos. (We didn't have money for an entertainment lawyer, but we would "copyright" them by sending the lyrics to the songs to ourselves in registered mail.) Then I would go, on my own, to record companies in Manhattan and try to get them to accept my demo and listen to it. I just went and knocked on doors. Sometimes it worked, sometimes it didn't.

Occasionally, I could find a connection to exploit. The big success was getting an audience with Nick Kalliongis at Arista Records. (Hey, I was also a Greek named Nick! How was he gonna say no?) He listened to our six-song demo, and then sat me down to talk.

"There is one song on this demo that's good," he said. "We can't begin to think about giving you a deal until you have three or four more songs that are this good."

I already knew the song he meant. It was called "Being With You." It was exciting to hear Nick leaving the door open for us, but at the same time, my heart sank. Writing that song had been capturing lightning in a bottle. A onetime thing. I knew we didn't have three or four more of those. (Of course, in the weeks after my meeting with Nick, we tried and tried to replicate it, to craft other songs on that level, but we never could.)

It became increasingly clear that if music was going to happen for me, it wasn't going to happen quickly. I was impatient for success. For this reason, I gravitated away from music after high school and moved on to other things. Also, I always knew that whatever I did, I wanted to be "the main guy." Being a drummer in a band is great, but let's face it, you're not the main guy!

Looking back at it now, I'm still kind of in awe of how brazen I was. How many high school kids would hop the LIRR to Manhattan with twenty demo tapes and just go door to door? (And even when I wasn't given an audience, I'd usually find a way to drop the cassette tape on the desk of somebody in A&R.)

> You never know when something in your life is going to come full circle. I thought my music industry days were long past, but now I'm using my experience to create opportunities for another person!

There were lessons in rejection for me as a young man. Yet as I've gone along, I've also seen that life can circle back in strange ways. Just because a business or occupation is "not for you" at one juncture doesn't mean it'll always be that way. (Believe it or not, Nick Kalliongis and I became friends and are still in touch to this day.)

Here's how it circled back for me . . .

In 2010, I invested in a YouTube marketing company with a guy named Christian "Murder" Murphy. This company would create our own YouTube stars and then sell advertising. Some of our successes were people like hip-hop artist Mike Stud, who now sells out 5,000-seat stages. Some of our stars we found just from basement demo tapes. Some, like the singer Jax, had finished second on American Idol. Jax also got to perform with Steven Tyler. (Later, unfortunately, I would have to break ties with Murphy because he proved himself to be a scoundrel, but that's another story.)

I started this simply as an interesting side hustle, but it did make some money. It had ups and downs. Some artists were profitable, and some weren't.

Fast-forward several years, and we got focused on this artist named Kiahra. She's a singer and songwriter who plays the piano. I discovered her, and when the YouTube company began to wind down, I continued to manage her. During the process, I found—all these many years since taking tapes to record companies in Manhattan— that I still really enjoyed working in the music industry and helping out artists I believed in.

For her part, Kiahra believed in me because I had discovered her. As it happened, I would have to draw on all of my previous experience to help her through the ups and downs of the industry.

Initially, I got her signed to Vincent Herbert, the guy who discovered Lady Gaga. (Some say it was technically Akon who discovered Gaga, but if that version is correct, Akon then handed her right to Vincent Herbert.) Vincent listened to Kiahra and brought her to L.A., where she performed for L.A. Reid. She played piano and sang for him. As the story goes, after she finished playing her seventh song, L.A. Reid leaped up and said, "Welcome to Arista Records. Welcome to the family!"

Just like that, things were happening. I felt pleased, not just for Kiahra and her career, but because I was helping to work deals in the record industry. Even if it wasn't my band being signed, I still enjoyed it vicariously!

So we worked out the terms, and L.A. Reid and his people were drawing up contracts for a big record deal with a million-dollar signing bonus. So then what happens? Reid gets fired for sexual harassment. Reid was out, and so were most of his projects. To be clear, sexual harassment has no place in any industry. It has to be taken seriously. But at the same time, did it make sense to punish Kiahra?

This was just as painful and challenging as you might imagine. We went back to Vincent, who promised he would be able to help us find another deal, but his own life had just gone into a tailspin. He'd lost TV shows and projects and was going through a very difficult divorce. It soon became clear he wasn't going to be able to do anything more for us. We had come so close, and now it wasn't going to happen. Kiahra and I were both so crushed. For a moment, I actually gave up—but only for a moment! I knew we had to keep trying.

Kiahra kept writing and recording outstanding music and sharing it online. I played her records for everyone I could find, and that included my partner Robert Cummins at Brooklyn Chop House. He had a long and storied history in the music industry that went all the way back to being childhood friends with the Notorious B.I.G. One day I was with Robert in his car, and I put on a song by Kiahra, one of her originals.

After just a few moments, Robert let out a "What the . . ."

And he literally pulled over to the side of the road.

"What the fuck is *that*?" he finished.

I told Robert who she was, and also the whole saga with L.A. Reid.

"I'm still representing her," I added. "Nobody is giving me another chance at a million-dollar advance because I'm not in the recording business. But you know, they might do it for *you*."

I'd seen how guests in the music industry treated Robert when they came to Brooklyn Chop House. They knew the deals he had made for so many people and always showed him the most respect.

I continued: "You've seen how amazing Kiahra is. Would you want to help me take one more shot at getting her in front of the right people?"

Robert was excited to see what he could do, so he connected us with D'Mile, the award-winning producer. (Robert had actually helped D'Mile get his start, putting him on a Mary J. Blige album that went platinum.) Just like that, D'Mile sent over three amazing, finished songs that he had been setting aside for major artists he worked with. D'Mile liked Kiahra so much and respected Robert so much that he just let us have them.

Now we'd been recording for nine months, and Kiahra had a record deal. She was signed by Irving Azoff—a hero of mine and one of the top three most powerful people in music. I'll never forget seeing the email in which Azoff had written: "Whatever you do, sign this girl!"

Shawn Holiday, who works for Azoff, came to hear Kiahra play and signed her to a new label named Giant Records that will launch in 2022. At the time of this writing, Kiahra has a publishing deal with Giant worth a quarter-million, and we're negotiating the terms of the rest of it. (I have to thank my attorney Paul Schindler for helping with this deal, because without him, nothing would have been possible. Paul is famous because he once charged Madonna only $1 as a retainer when she was starting out—and Madonna didn't have the money, so he loaned her the dollar, too!) The paperwork is now with the legal team, but we're hopeful that Kiahra's record deal will soon get over the finish line. Don't be surprised if you see her at next year's Grammy Awards. She's that good!

As you can imagine, I'm so happy for Kiahra, and so honored that she allowed me to be her sherpa as we took this journey together. (I should note that Kiahra is one of those people who are going to be successful no matter what—it's just a question of how soon somebody in the industry sees it. Just on her own, as an unsigned artist, she had about 100,000 Instagram followers, and videos of her performing have over 3 million views. She shoots everything on her iPhone, and I'm already in touch with them about doing some advertising for them with Kiahra, after her record comes out, where she can say: "I got signed with what I recorded on my iPhone." Because it's true!)

I'm a guy who wanted to get a record deal in the early eighties when I was just a kid. And now I'm finally making it happen for someone near and dear to me. It's a great feeling. That's because of persistence, not giving up, and never assuming I was done with a particular industry. Sometimes all it takes is making a connection to the right person, like my partner Robert, in this case, to push something over the finish line.

TAKEAWAYS FOR FUTURE DISRUPTORS

- **Disruptors give back and use their success to help cultivate the next generation.**
- **For ill or good, disruptors must engage with the communities that have allowed them to be successful.**
- **You may be done with an industry, but that doesn't mean it's done with you!**

CHAPTER THIRTEEN:

This Is What Happens to Dishonorable Men and Women

I'm not that old, but I've worked in the hospitality industry long enough to observe the arc of the universe. You don't have to be the keenest observer to see that those who go through life betraying others usually wind up in very bad places. Yet at the same time, those who prove themselves loyal can garner great reward. This chapter is about how I've seen that work in my own life. Every disruptor should understand that justice is rarely swift, but it does come eventually. If or when you are betrayed, your betrayer may not face punishment immediately. Hell, it may look like they're never going to face consequences for what they did to you. But give things a little bit of time. Devils have a way of getting their due . . .

After Mike Reda and Robert Darby got bought out of Philippe, they took one of the head chefs from Philippe and opened their own Asian restaurant called Red Stixs (yes, that's how they spelled "sticks"). To make this happen, Mike Reda went to investors and essentially did an impersonation of *me*! He presented himself as the founder and creator of Philippe and claimed everything surrounding it had been his idea. The business plan. The menu. The marketing.

And now he had a *new* restaurant in the works . . . so would they like to invest?

This kind of move was not a surprise, given what I knew of Mike Reda.

It was lying and fraud. At the same time, Reda correctly understood that no one was going to call him on it—at least not initially. The investors *wanted* to believe him, and so they did. They threw in millions of dollars to help Mike Reda and Robert Darby open Red Stixs.

And guess what? It was a complete bomb.

It failed *precisely because* Mike Reda and Robert Darby couldn't do what I could. They were razzle-dazzle men with the investors, but they lacked the real skill set and know-how. They didn't have the years of growing up in the restaurant industry that I had.

The food at Red Stixs was actually not terrible, but Mike and Robert had just assumed that with pretty good food, people would march into their restaurant the moment the doors opened. It didn't happen.

Red Stixs struggled from the start and never stopped struggling. After a while, it became unable to pay its rent. That situation went on for over a year. Seeing the writing on the wall, Mike Reda began quietly pocketing hundreds of thousands of dollars for himself out of what meager profits there were. It turned out he had a serious gambling problem he needed to feed, and he'd kept this problem a secret from everyone he knew. Reda's problem went so deep that the Hard Rock Casino had given him his own assigned private parking space!

(As an aside, I've seen so many people go bad with gambling addiction as a driving force behind it. To give just other example, I had a second cousin named Frankie to whom I gave a job as VP of operations at the Philippe Chow in Miami. He also house-sat my Florida home for me. One day he called to tell me my house had been burglarized . . . but it later turned out he had staged a fake break-in and sold all of my appliances. Not content with that, as I eventually learned, when another employee was fired, he would secretly keep them on the payroll and cash their paychecks himself using a fake ID. All to fund a degenerate gambling habit!)

Anyhow, as Red Stixs continued to sputter, Mike Reda stole about $800,000 from the restaurant for himself. Then he called up all of his oldest, lifelong friends in the business world—people like Jerry Sbarro (of Sbarro pizza)—and told them he was looking to sell points at Red Stixs. (He presented Red Stixs as profitable, when of course it was a mess that hadn't been able to pay rent for a year!) So he got several hundred thousand dollars that way, too.

And here comes the kicker!

Simultaneously, Mike Reda sold his own mother's house—*without her knowing it was happening!*—for another $500,000!

Then he took all of that money and disappeared. Nobody ever heard from him again.

Word soon circulated that his tales of having a brain tumor were a lie. Officially, his family members said that he left the United States for Germany to get brain tumor treatment there. But either way, he was gone from the face of the Earth. Disappeared. Vanished. A bunch of people he owed money to were looking for him—and this included some connected guys.

Pretty soon, his wife, who was still stateside working as a real estate broker, started saying that Mike had died of cancer and was buried in Germany. The funny thing is, there's no record of a funeral service or burial, and none of Mike's other family members know anything about

> A guy who will fake a brain tumor will do a lot of other horrible things. When people show you who they are, believe them!

this. Then, about five years after Mike disappeared—*boom!* His wife is suddenly gone, too. She's just gone. There one day and gone the next. (Information I have leads me to believe that Mike Reda is currently living under an assumed identity in Cuba, working at a casino-hotel. We'll see if the future proves me right on that!)

But in the meantime, Red Stixs went under completely. This time, it was Robert Darby with the PG (personal guarantee), left holding the bag. He was forced to declare bankruptcy. And it all collapsed. If you ask me, these guys got just what they deserved!

I'm not a good judge of godfathers for my kids. From Mike Reda to Michael Gabriel, I'm 0-for-2. Both are godfathers to my daughters, and both betrayed me. Both backstabbed me. And both are extremely troubled men today, down to their very souls.

Here's another little story: My daughter's favorite dish is chicken satay. When I was out after Philippe, she wanted to order twenty chicken satays for her birthday celebration from Red Stixs. Mike Reda was running it then, of course, and he refused to fill the order. This was a ten-year-old girl we're talking about at this point. Can you imagine that? And his own goddaughter to boot!

* * *

Here's another illustrative tale for future disruptors. Back when I opened Ciano, I had built that restaurant around a chef named Shea

Gallante. He was very tight with Hassan Mohammed, who was the landlord at the restaurant, and unbeknownst to me, Hassan had plans with Bruce Eichner to knock down the building one day. The place had a demolition clause, but I'd been told he would not exercise it for at least ten years. Looking back, Gallante must have known the demo would be sooner.

Shea Gallante's other problem was that he had a 40 percent kitchen payroll and a 40 percent food cost, when a successful restaurant should have had 15 percent kitchen payroll and 30 percent food cost. Because of this discrepancy, I knew something was wrong. I just wasn't sure what . . .

> **Trust your instinct when something seems off at your business. That's a lesson I learned from my dad!**

Every time I would tell him to get these numbers in order, he would threaten to walk out and take the rest of the staff with him if I didn't get off his back. And we'd just gotten two stars in the *New York Times* and three stars in *Bloomberg*. The place was critically acclaimed, and we were putting out beautiful plates. However, the costs were so high, we weren't making the money we should have been.

Then, in a flash, all was revealed . . .

I came into the restaurant at six in the morning one day, and I found coolers full of pasta made with our pasta maker. I asked the guys on duty at the time what this was. They said, "Oh, it's being delivered."

It turned out it was being delivered to another restaurant that Shea Gallante had opened in Armonk, New York. He was using our food, our pasta chefs, and our kitchen to prepare food to serve later in his Armonk restaurant. I had been absorbing food costs for a restaurant that I had nothing to do with. And *that* was why our food costs were always so high!

I'd caught him red-handed, and I confronted him.

Shea said, "I'm only doing this because you promised me more money than I'm getting."

"No, Shea," I said. "I promised you more money if you kept your food cost and payroll costs in line, which you never did. You're about 100 percent over the industry norm, which will put us out of business. Then, on top of that, you decided to steal."

At that point, I was done. I just surrendered the lease and closed the place. At the end of the day, I didn't put up a big fight. It's unfortunate, because we were doing $5 million a year, but you can't make money even with that kind of income if people are stealing from you left and right. The lesson I learned there is: Never build your entire brand around a chef. I thought I'd learned that lesson with Philippe Chow, but apparently not! (Since then, Shea has failed at everything he's done—at least as an entrepreneur. Now he works for someone else.)

* * *

Another tale of deception involves Dara Mirjahangiry. Dara worked for me at Philippe, and I knew him for many years. He started as a waiter at Philippe and gradually rose through the ranks.

When I opened Jue Lan—the venue that replaced the Limelight—he came to me asking for a job. I gave him a job as a manager, and over time he grew to be a GM. When I left Jue Lan, Dara stayed behind. Then he worked at Red Stixs for a while.

And to be honest, I lost track of him after that.

But in January 2022, I heard through the grapevine that he was opening up his own restaurant, an Asian fusion place called Sei Less. I called him up to wish him well.

At times, Dara had been like my protégé, a guy I tried to teach all the tricks of the trade. But I was about to learn that Dara had broken the #1 rule in my business: Never betray the person who brought you up the ladder.

When I investigated Sei Less, I learned that Dara had copied Brooklyn Chop House pretty much 1:1. The touches he had stolen were brazen, from the menu to the decor to the advertising.

Then, the real betrayal.

I started seeing interviews with Dara in the press in which he called Sei Less the "brainchild" of Philippe Chow and Jue Lan. Whatever that means. But those are two places that I created. He was making it sound as though he had created them.

It was time for another phone call.

"Dara," I told him over the phone, "I'm very upset by what you're saying in the press. Your statement implies things that are not true. You were not the brains behind any of these places; you just worked there. You're making me into an enemy. Do you want that?"

"It was all the PR firm!" Dara insisted. "They put those things in my mouth when they wrote the press release."

But here's the thing: Dara was an owner now. He was responsible for everything, including how he was quoted. Nothing happened—and certainly no press release got sent—without his okay. Dara had not yet realized that when you're an owner, you don't get to blame others like that. The buck stops with you. If your PR team sent out something with incorrect wording, it was your fault for not insisting that you approve the quote.

When you become an owner, you've got to act like one.

I contacted the media outlets that had run the stories implying Dara was the guy behind Philippe and Jue Lan, and, to their credit, they understood the situation and redacted everything.

And I told Dara that in my opinion, Sei Less could be called Sei Lies! If the magazines covering the restaurant had wanted to print the truth, they would have reported *these* facts: "Former server at Philippe

Chow and manager at Jue Lan—who also participated in the failed venture, Red Stixs—opens new restaurant."

By trying to take credit for things that I had done, Dara was figuratively slapping me in the face, because I had been the source of all his opportunities (or at least the opportunities where he'd had any success). Never burn someone who helped you up the ladder. I helped Dara go from server to GM to owner. And this was how he repaid me.

As an entrepreneur and disruptor, you may find yourself in situations where you have to compete against your former mentors. That's perfectly okay, *as long as you compete fairly.* By misrepresenting himself and his business to the press, Dara had chosen another route.

> Some people are so vile they're best left forgotten. The only way they "win" is if you continue to expend energy thinking about them.

Betrayal is painful, but you also have to decide how much energy to waste on it. I stopped expending energy after I got the papers to retract the untruths Dara had sent them. Morally bankrupt people can be infuriating, but you can't let yourself get too distracted by it. It's too much of a time and energy suck. Fix the situation, then let it go!

* * *

Let me end this chapter with a note about someone who is not a devil at all. I would hate for the reader to think that I only remember the people I work with when some kind of betrayal is involved. In just as many, if not more, cases, there are feel-good stories of loyalty and growth in my life.

One of these would be Peter Olcan. I was able to help Peter grow his career from a server to a host, to a floor manager, to a GM, to a director of operations at Brooklyn Dumpling Shops. Without his help, there is no way I'd be at over 100 stores right now.

The key for me with Peter is that I was able to see that he understood technology so well. I knew he was a guy who was happy to put in eighteen-hour days, but the fact that he was technically minded as well has allowed us to do wonderful things together.

Actually, when I was in the process of interviewing people to be the director of operations, Peter was by my side interviewing them. And at one point he just turned to me and said, "Hey, you know, I could do this if you give me the opportunity."

And you know what? He was right. And I did give him the opportunity. It has worked out wonderfully for both of us. Now Peter has an amazing career and an *extremely* bright future!

For every Dara, there are about five Peters!

TAKEAWAYS FOR FUTURE DISRUPTORS

- **Over time, for good or ill, people will show you who they are.**
- **Devils get their due . . . but so do loyal friends.**

CHAPTER FOURTEEN:

Disruptors Should Always Run toward the Burning Building

Aspiring disruptors have quite a bit to learn from what happened to the economy during COVID. There has probably been no more illustrative, instructional event in my lifetime. COVID times have proved that it is possible—and, indeed, sometimes much easier—to disrupt existing models and create success during times of crisis. If you are truly a disruptor, you will have an innate sense of this. Couple that sense with courage, and you will take the steps necessary to benefit from a crisis. You'll run toward the burning building, instead of away from it.

I've said it before and I'll say it again: If you want to be a disruptor, you have to be the kind of person who will run toward the burning building, not away from it.

COVID was a burning building that burned people, livelihoods, and entire industries. But it was also a catalyst for incredible acts of kindness. It was a source of incredible opportunities for people who knew where to look for them. And its impact will forever be tied to the tale of my own businesses.

When the pandemic hit, I started getting calls from every major landlord in New York City looking to give me a deal on a closed restaurant. I gave them a hard "no" about 99 percent of the time. But when Rick Friedland from Friedland Properties called me, he had something different.

"Stratis," he said, "Buffalo Wild Wings just handed in the keys on a 25,000-square-foot restaurant in the heart of Times Square!"

"Rick," I said, "with all due respect, these kinds of deals aren't for me. These deals—these locations—are only for the big guys. I'm not going to be able to give you the guarantees that you need on your lease for a

> When someone makes you an offer, it never hurts to take a look!

place like that. In that part of town, anyone with a lease on a space over 6,000 square feet is a public company."

But Rick was insistent.

"Just come and see the space," he said.

So I did.

The space had forty-eight-foot ceilings, a rooftop bar and dining room, five interior dining rooms, and more! Seriously, it was a masterpiece of restaurant design. I want to give props to Buffalo Wild Wings; they'd done an amazing job creating the space.

Rick told me BWW had put $15 million in the space back in 2016. Now he wanted me to turn it into a second Brooklyn Chop House. (Two years later, I would joke with Mayor Eric Adams that he should give me the key to the city because my restaurants got rid of the last Denny's and the last Buffalo Wild Wings in Manhattan!)

It was incredibly tempting, but I hadn't been exaggerating with Rick on the phone. This was the kind of space normally only available to much, much bigger guys.

I laid out what my terms would have to be.

"Rick," I said, "I could do 8 percent capped at $1.1 million." This was my business partner Robert "Don Pooh" Cummins's great idea. It meant that I would pay 8 percent of my gross sales after taxes as rent. If I did a million dollars' worth of business, Rick would get $80,000 of rent for that year. If I did $12 million or above, Rick would still only get $1.1 million in rent; that would be the cap. (I thought the landlord would never possibly agree to this, but he did!) There would also be a "base rent" of $35,000 a month.

I told Rick I would need a "COVID clause," too. That would stipulate that if the government were to shut us down or limit our capacity due to COVID, and if we were not covered by insurance, then we'd revert to an 8 percent lease *with no base rent.*

But here's the thing: I knew that with COVID gone, this location would be able to do amazing business. I thought $35 million would be well within the realm of possibility.

In the end, Rick and I worked out a twenty-year lease agreement. My guaranteed minimum on the lease would be just $80,000. Most guaranteed leases for places in Times Square range from $5–20 million! (At the time of this writing, Brooklyn Chop House in Times Square is just days away from opening.)

Part of the digital assets that came with the lease on the space was an $800,000 digital billboard in the heart of Times Square. I can put anything on it that I want to: Sponsorships! Advertisements! Anything!

I earn about $30,000 a month from the advertising. I can also use it to advertise

> **Times of crisis can change everything. What used to be way beyond your scope might now be a real possibility!**

our own restaurants or allow customers to feature special custom messages: "Welcome JP Morgan Holiday Party!" or "Will you marry me?" or "Happy Birthday!" The possibilities are endless!

A billboard like that, in this location, is normally far beyond the means of little guys like me!

* * *

As this was going on, a real estate developer named Sean Lefkowitz contacted me and said: "Hey, I just bought this building, and I want you to put in a Brooklyn Chop House."

(I should note that although Sean made the phone call, this deal ultimately came to me through James Famularo of Meridian Capital Group, a real estate broker I've worked with for years. He would always call me before things went on the market to other restaurateurs; James has always had my back. Working with him, I ended up doing two of the biggest restaurant deals during all of COVID.)

Anyhow, I told Sean I couldn't do that because I was really close to closing a deal in Times Square.

But the thing was, I'd always wanted to bring back Pappas, my grandfather's old restaurant. It had closed in 1975. When my grandfather and my granduncles passed away, Pappas didn't make it through the next generation. (And to compound my misery, a bunch of imitators then copied the name Pappas!)

So Sean showed me this really awesome space, right in the heart of Greenwich Village. I start thinking: "Maybe it's time to bring Pappas back to the Morfogen family . . ."

I knew I didn't want to do the status quo Greek restaurant. I didn't want to do the old Pappas menu from 1910. I wanted to do my own version of it. I wanted to call the new place Pappas Taverna, and I wanted it to have a wood-burning Greek oven where we could do traditional Greek cooking (which actually uses an oven, not a grill). I also wanted to bring some of my Asian restaurant influence into it—for example, table-slicing a gyro the way you would a Peking duck. I knew this place could do a lot of things that haven't been seen before in the traditional Greek restaurant.

After securing the space from Sean, I partnered with chef Peter Spyropoulos. He was the chef at Milos and studied under David Bouley. He's one of the top Greek chefs in the country. I also wanted my brother, Nick, to help me out a little bit. Nick is the master of the wood-burning oven and is consulting with us on meat and fish and traditional Greek dishes. We'll do casseroles in a wood-burning oven. It's time to bring that back!

And we're going to disrupt and reimagine, too . . .

Desserts will be redone as spring rolls. I'm doing the baklava as spring rolls with filo dough. I don't want Peter copying the dishes from the places he's already worked; I want him coming in and disrupting desserts! I want him swimming in his own lane. I want him doing duck pâté honey puffs with dried cherries. I want him doing avocado tzatziki.

And the most fun, most disruptive thing of all will be doing a half-bottle wine program. Any bottle from $60 up to $2,000, you'll be able to order a half-bottle or have it by the glass. Let's say you only want a glass of wine from a $2,000 bottle. We'll sell you a glass for $500! Or a half-bottle for $1,000. Nobody has ever done this to that extent. There will be glasses of wine for $12, but also for $500!

With my brother, Nick, and Pappas Taverna disrupting the Greek restaurant industry—with all of these changes I've described, including being the first wood-burning Greek restaurant on the planet—it shows the way that my family's vision has finally come full circle. As we're positioned now, Pappas is going to disrupt it all!

* * *

The darkest part of COVID for me was probably the passing of my own mother.

My mother was one of only eleven people to die from the COVID vaccine in New York. It was after the second Moderna shot. She was gardening later in the day after getting the shot and called me and told me her knees hurt. A week after that, she suddenly collapsed in her kitchen.

The hospital first diagnosed severe arthritis. But the truth was the Moderna vaccine had given her Guillain-Barré syndrome. It caused her body's own immune system to attack her nerves.

When they finally realized what was happening, they tried blood transfusions to get the vaccine out of her system, but it was too late. After six transfusions, she passed away. The antibodies had attacked her spinal column and paralyzed her body, resulting in her death.

After this happened, the federal government got in touch and offered my family a settlement of $250,000. (Not many people know this, but a fund has been put aside for the families of people who die from the vaccine.) We did not accept this money, because it appeared to come with conditions that amounted to a "gag order" when it came to discussing what had happened. I told them to shove that money—and the gag order—up their ass!

The government doesn't want people talking about the fact that too many antibodies can kill you. My mother had too many, probably because she had already had COVID and had recovered, and had never known it. Taking the second Moderna vaccine was essentially an overdose of antibodies.

I'm now in the process of filing a lawsuit against the hospital that treated my mother. I've hired Sanford Rubenstein and Ira Newman as my lawyers. We are suing the hospital for an incorrect diagnosis of arthritis. Even with her reaction, it might have been possible for them to save her. And yet they took four weeks just to do a spinal tap and find out what was wrong. Beside money, I'm going to get them to admit what they did to her.

I share this because I think this tragic situation of my mom's passing speaks to the disruptor model in an important way. These people initially told me it was just arthritis. In the back of my mind, I knew it wasn't going to be arthritis. I had to push and push the whole time just to eventually get them to make the correct diagnosis, albeit tragically too late to save my mother. If I had been more disruptive, if I had pushed even harder, if I hadn't waited to see the head of the department . . . then who knows?

> Throughout your life, various powerful entities will insist that you "sit back and take it" when it comes to the status quo. A disruptor is always prepared to resist . . . especially when it comes to things concerning their family.

A disruptor has to refuse to accept the status quo. A disruptor has to question what they are told and ask, "How do you know this?" even when dealing with experts. A disruptor must have, always, at the front of their minds, the readiness and willingness to disrupt the accepted systems being forced upon them.

During COVID, I think there was the attitude among healthcare providers that someone who is eighty or older can basically be discarded. If they pass away for any reason during this time, it isn't a big deal. That's a way of thinking that damn sure needs to be disrupted!

* * *

I'm very proud of how my daughter Beatrice has been able to navigate COVID. She got it when she was just fifteen years old, in November of 2020. She spent hours with the tracers, giving careful accounts of everyone she'd been in direct or indirect contact with.

Despite this, she started getting bullied on TikTok and Snapchat. These kids were posting awful messages like "Fuck you, Bea. It's your fault I can't go out this weekend, just because you said I was somewhere you were."

They were bullying my daughter to the point where it started to make her feel depressed. As a parent, I was concerned and upset.

I had a conversation with her, and I said: "You know, Bea, take a lesson from your dad. Right now, you think you're down and out, but we're going to take this and make something good out of it. We're going to make lemonade out of lemons. We're going to stand up to COVID cyberbullying. What these kids are doing is wrong. We're going to fight against it because you're not the only kid experiencing it. You did everything correctly. These kids can't be allowed to treat you like this."

Simultaneously, I got a phone call from a friend of my daughter's parents. They wanted to chew me out for letting my daughter be where their child had been. But they had confused the timeline and were talking about an event that had happened three days before my daughter knew she was positive. But they didn't care; they wanted somebody to yell at!

"I just got a double mastectomy, and we live with our ninety-year-old mother!" this woman screamed at me. "If anything happens to her, I'm gonna hold you responsible!"

> Disrupt a negative by turning it into a positive whenever you can. If my daughter can do it, so can you!

It was crazy. It was also a threat, and I ended up calling the press on these people.

But what my daughter did next was really lovely! She created an Instagram account (with the tag #virusisourenemy) dedicated to stopping bullying related to COVID and reminding people that the virus is the enemy. She got on the front cover of *Newsday* with it! Endorsements came in from far and wide, including from the mayor of New York City. She also did an interview about it on Fox News.

I was so happy because my daughter had been able to find a purpose in what she was going through and turn it into something that would help out other people who might be going through the same thing. She had become an advocate, and, even more important, she had become a disruptor. She was thinking about things in a whole new way, disrupting a culture of bullying, and helping others. She did Zooms with groups all over the world about her experience.

During COVID, I saw a lot of restaurateur friends of mine go through hard times—and I mean big brands, big names!

One of these was a friend of mine who owns Serafina Pizza and Farinella Pizza, both of which have multiple locations in New York.

The owners approached me and were like, "Hey, we see in the press that you're opening all these locations and doing deals for Brooklyn Dumpling Shop products with Walmart. Can you help us out? We've got a brand that's thirty-five years old, and we're just in four supermarkets."

I said, "I love you guys, and I'm going to do everything I can to help you."

I introduced Serafina Pizza to Patti LaBelle's group. To make a long story short, now they're also slated to hit 1,000 Walmarts by the end of this year.

I did this simply to help my friends. They needed help because they really needed to diversify. That's a lesson for all entrepreneurs: Diversify, diversify, diversify. Even though you may have a steady restaurant business, you need to grow your consumer goods products whenever possible. You need to make sure that if one industry collapses, you'll set yourself up to have revenue from other sources.

Now Serafina is building a new location in Newark, New Jersey's Penn Station called Gateway. And there, they received a Tenant Improvement Allowance for millions of dollars to build out the space based on my relationship with Jonathan Schultz from Onyx. I'm just giving my resources to a friend in need.

After the Walmart deal was squared away, they came back to me and said, "We also just took over a brand called Farinella Pizza. It's known as the pizza you can buy by the foot, and it's delicious."

So I said, "This is very franchisable," and I helped them get a deal to franchise their pizza.

Helping people like that is kind of my drug. I want to help others, and I also want to share the tactics that I know can help them diversify. Now they've got their traditional restaurants, they've got franchising, and they've got frozen food for sale in stores.

I couldn't be happier than when I help a friend!

TAKEAWAYS FOR FUTURE DISRUPTORS

- **Always run into the burning building; it's literally a fire sale.**
- **If you're not the kind of disruptor who will go to bat for your family and friends, you're nothing!**

CHAPTER FIFTEEN:

Disrupt a Crisis by Doing the Right Thing

In addition to creating opportunities for disruptors to grow their businesses and cash in on a fire sale, the pandemic also illustrated the duty that we have to do the right thing and create positive change in the world. When a crisis occurs, 99 percent of people feel concerned but will wait for an authority figure like the government to tell them what to do. But the 1 percent who are disruptors will simply act. We will immediately ask ourselves how we can help people during the crisis, and then we'll follow through with action. We disrupt the model that says that charity, philanthropy, or assistance must flow through certain established channels. Instead, we see the problem and we solve the problem. And let me tell you something, those who give get something in return. Acts of kindness are remembered. During the direst of times, they're remembered forever. This chapter will make clear why disruptors should never wait to be told what to do by the government but should instead trust their own experience and wisdom to get the job done.

C OVID tested everyone who worked in my industry. At Brooklyn Chop House, when the pandemic first hit, we had to decide what to do with this situation.

I said to my partners, "We have one restaurant at this moment. I want to be able to look back at this time and be proud of ourselves. I want to tell my grandkids that we did something special!"

After a little brainstorming, we decided that we would start donating meals to New York Presbyterian Hospital, which was just a two-minute walk from Brooklyn Chop House. We started by delivering twenty to thirty packages of food a night. Everything from lobster and steaks to chicken and fish. We did this every night and asked for zero recognition. Even so, the doctors and nurses started posting "Thank You" signs and messages to us on Instagram. They would use hashtags like #BrooklynChopHouseThankYou. And we would always respond, "No, you guys are the heroes. Thank *YOU*!"

> **Nobody knows how you can positively impact a situation better than YOU! The government doesn't know your capabilities. Neither do politicians. But YOU do!**

Then Jen Keil from the *New York Post* saw that this was going on and ran a story calling me "the hero of the day."

But I wasn't a hero. I was just reacting to the situation. Early in the pandemic, I chanced to visit the Emergency Department of a hospital. I couldn't believe what I was seeing. I couldn't believe how everyone from janitorial staff to doctors and nurses were so willing to put their lives at risk for the good of the city. People were putting in eighteen-to-twenty-hour shifts to fight a virus we still knew very little about. And these people had families. This boggled my mind. They were like war heroes.

But when that article about me came out, I got contacted by Sysco Foods, Forever Young wines, Junior's Cheesecake, For Five Coffee, Voss water, and all these other brands asking how they could help me out. They wanted to be a part of what we were doing at Brooklyn Chop House. I soon filled up my entire restaurant with their donated products. They sent me thousands of boxes of food and beverages. Simultaneously, I was fielding calls from about twenty hospitals asking if there was a way I could help start a program to recognize and support their staff. And of course, I said, "Sure!"

I gathered all the supporters, and we began a program that over the course of six months greatly expanded the amount of philanthropy we could provide. From March through July, we donated over 8,400 meals to nineteen hospitals, three police departments, and a nursing home. We would get calls all the time from businesses big and small wanting to donate things.

We also had people contacting us asking if we had a GoFundMe to support Brooklyn Chop House employees. I told these folks we didn't use donation pages like that, but what they could do was commit to coming and eating at our restaurant when we were able to reopen. That's what would allow me to hire my staff back. We don't want you to buy gift cards or start GoFundMe pages—though we so appreciate the sentiment—we want you to come and eat at our restaurant when we reopen.

You'd think restaurants like mine would be rewarded for this self-lessness with a clear and logical path to reopen and preserve our businesses. Instead, the complete opposite seemed to happen.

In May, Governor Cuomo said restaurants would be allowed to reopen July 1, but on June 30, he said he was changing his mind and restaurants would not be allowed to open after all. I personally know of about 100 New York restaurants that went out of business just because of the reversal of that order. Cuomo didn't know the restaurant industry, and he thought opening a restaurant was like turning on a light switch. It's not. It takes two to three weeks of investing in perishables and nonperishables, training, staffing, and cleaning. And you have to pay the staff while you are training them.

But Cuomo, in an act I consider essentially criminal, shut things down the day before restaurants were ready to open for indoor dining. Businesses like mine had been investing in things like glass dividers and UV lights to keep everyone

> Even in leading global cities, the government will reliably propose regulations in areas it knows nothing about! Always be ready for that.

extremely safe. So much money had been spent by restaurants all across the city. (Personally, I had invented my own temperature check device that combined a thermometer with a walkthrough frame from a metal detector. It was very accurate and worked much better than leaning into someone's forehead with a temperature gun. If you were over 99.5, it would let you know you weren't allowed to enter!)

Cuomo proved the axiom that most politicians have never run a lemonade stand, much less a small business! When they start making decisions that impact small businesses, it's usually a recipe for disaster.

That was the moment I started calling the governor "Comrade Cuomo" whenever I spoke to the media. In my opinion, he and Mayor "De Lousio" are two of the worst things ever to happen to New York City, and that includes Bin Laden. Now, that's a statement I've made before, and whenever I say it, people get kind of cautious and diplomatic and say things like, "That's a strong opinion, Stratis."

It's not just a "strong opinion." They killed about thirteen thousand people in nursing homes though their incompetent policies. People in nursing homes, many of whom didn't even have COVID yet, got it from overcrowding because the governor and mayor were stubborn and didn't want to use the federal resources available to them.

Even Cuomo's own data suggested that 74.5 percent of the spread was coming from home gatherings, and 1.5 percent was occurring at restaurants. Now remember, he was also asking restaurants to trace everything, and to collect customer phone and email for this purpose. Shopping malls, big box stores, airports, and other places of congregation were not compelled to do this—but we were! Restaurants were an easy target, and so we were targeted.

Entities like The New York City Hospitality Alliance, which should have been advocating for us, proved useless during this time. They were supposed to be our voice, and yet they did nothing. Andrew Riggie and Robert Bookman, who run it, did the opposite of protecting our industry. To this day, I am so upset at how they acted. They did zero to protect restaurants. In my opinion, Riggie and Bookman thought only of themselves and never wanted to be brave and risk upsetting their Albany connections. Consequently, the rights of restaurants and restaurant workers were trampled on by Cuomo and De Blasio. (I've said it to Riggie and Bookman right to their faces, but I'll say it here again: After how they acted, I would never be a part of The New York City Hospitality Alliance or sit on its board. Never.)

So, in July of 2020, restaurants were allowed to open *outdoors only*.

We did that, and what happened at Brooklyn Chop House was amazing. Our business went from $80,000 a week in the summer of 2019 to over $250,000 a week *just with outdoor seating* in the summer of 2020. This was because people had been listening when I'd told

> Kindness and philanthropy have a way of being rewarded—especially for disruptors who didn't hesitate to do the right thing!

them the way to support us was not with gift cards or online fundraisers, but by coming and eating at our restaurant. This was all the healthcare workers and their families coming to say thanks. There's a cliché that if you give to the community, they'll give back to you. I gotta be honest, I didn't really know if I believed that before July of 2020. Previously, I'd always tried to be a good member of the community, but I was never certain if that was translating to better business at my restaurants or not. But now there was no longer any doubt in my mind. What happened here was irrefutable proof that we did well by doing good. Our kindness came back to us a thousandfold, and suddenly we were doing a million dollars a month with only outdoor seating. It made me emotional because I never expected this kind of support, but I was so thankful for it because it enabled me to hire my staff back.

This brings me to the so-called leaders of our industry during this time, like Danny Meyer of Shake Shack. The big boys running our industry needed to behave better.

De Blasio, misinformed as he always is, said in 2021 that Danny Meyer set the benchmark for how businesses should act during times of crisis. I heard that and said, *"Really?"*

If I had 186 burger joins with a $2 billion market cap and $105 million in cash on hand, I wouldn't be applying for $10 million in PPP loans. Danny Meyer got that $10 million at a time when there were honest, struggling restaurateurs (many of whom I knew personally) who were dying trying to find just $100,000 to keep their little bistro in Brooklyn open, or their little bodega in Queens afloat.

Not only did Meyer get that $10 million, but he also got it by filling out 186 separate applications in order to stay under the five-hundred-employee rule. I don't know how anyone can look at that plain, stark fact and not determine that Meyer engaged in something intentionally deceptive and criminal.

Meyer showed who he truly was during this time. Sometimes people let you see who they really are, and Meyer sure did that during COVID. He should never again be called a leader of our industry, or of anything else positive for that matter.

Yet these are the people that goofs like De Blasio are saying we should look to for inspiration and put on a pedestal!

I wish I could tell De Blasio to his face, "No. *I* should be lauded as a leader of industry, because at a time when the Danny Meyers of the world thought only of themselves, I took a single restaurant and served thousands and thousands of healthcare heroes. Yet Meyer was the first to close, the first to lay off, and the first with his hand out for millions of dollars of taxpayer money . . . when he had $105 million on hand."

Worst of all, when Meyer gave the $10 million back—because he was called out by the president, and because #boycottshakeshack went viral—he was considered a hero. Now, if I had filled out 186 applications in order to stay under the radar and illegally get money through deception, I would be in jail today, and rightfully so!

One of the things I'd like to do as a disruptor is disrupt my whole fucking industry so that people with the moral compass of a Danny Meyer are never again a spokesperson for *our* industry. We should be ashamed to be associated with the likes of him.

If I had been in Danny Meyer's situation, I would have told my shareholders, "Look, we're gonna lose $40–50 million this year no matter what we do. So we're gonna open every Shake Shack and allow them to become free cafeterias for all the healthcare heroes. All 186 restaurants will stay open with people employed. Regular customers can come, but if you've got an ID from a hospital, you eat for free. And ladies and gentlemen, we're going to come out of this the most beloved restaurant brand in America. And from there, the sky's the limit." But did he have the foresight to do this? No, he didn't.

* * *

Cuomo and De Blasio continued to say that restaurants were not safe, even though all of the data—their own data—showed that the opposite was true. They reluctantly reopened indoor dining in September of 2020, only to close it in December, the most celebratory month of the year! Here's what's mind-boggling to me: How could they close down the restaurant industry in the biggest month of the year when all of these health safeguards and improvements have just been made? Everyone is tested, masked up, and safe.

At Brooklyn Chop House, we didn't merely do the twelve restaurant safety steps that Cuomo and De Blasio told restaurants to do: we did forty. Forty steps! Forty safety steps. I even offered them to Cuomo and De Blasio. As I once said to them on Fox News, "Take my forty steps and use them and get the restaurants back into commerce!"

> **The way disruptors do things can often create a model for the entire industry.**

Restaurants were so much safer than the alternative, which was people congregating in homes. Why—in the most celebratory month of the year, when everyone is going to be gathering and celebrating— would the government choose to drive people to gather in unsafe places? Now people were pushed into apartments. I had to kick people out of my restaurant at 10:00 p.m. on New Year's Eve so they could go watch De Blasio and his wife on TV as they danced in an empty Times Square; it looked like a cemetery! Let me tell you what people did after that . . . What they *didn't* do was go home to their apartments alone and go to bed. They started gathering in residences together and ordering food for delivery. These weren't romantic dinners for two; they were massive spreads for twenty to thirty people. I know this because I saw the massive orders go out the door. And I'm telling you, these apartments didn't have HEPA filters and masks! There was no temperature screening, and there were no dividers between groups.

At the time, I called it. Looking at those massive orders of food going out to big partiers, I realized this was going to create the sequel to the nursing home debacle. In January, we were going to see such a spike in this virus because everyone had been pushed to celebrate in homes.

And that, of course, is what happened.

Cuomo and De Blasio took steps that may have left them covered politically, but that seldom translated into meaningful progress on fighting COVID. The wave we got in January and February was all on Cuomo for shutting down the restaurants, as far as I'm concerned.

* * *

Also during COVID, I did a show on NBC called *Rebound* about businesses trying to bounce back from the pandemic. It profiled several entrepreneurs, and I was one of them. Whenever I spoke on the show, I made a point to call Cuomo "Comrade Cuomo." Then Fox News asked me to come on, and I did, sharing that in my opinion Cuomo and De Blasio hadn't figured out that by shutting down the economy—and shutting down the safe, sanitized, regulated places for people to congregate, like restaurants—they were doing the opposite of fighting the virus. They were doing the opposite of what epidemiologists recommended. They were taking the steps that would move us further from herd immunity, instead of toward it. By locking people into home gatherings, they were not just destroying livelihoods, but also doing the opposite of what should have been done to fight the virus. Now you had *both* a sick populace and a closed economy. And what does that lead to?

Suicide. Depression. Alcoholism. Drug addiction. Mental illness. Domestic violence. And street crime.

I predicted that all of these things would explode. That they would go from doubling to five or six times the norm. And you know what, I was right!

One of the saddest of these is crime. People in our society with criminal intent can use the mask mandates to get away with crimes.

Gangbangers and thugs know exactly what they are doing with masks. The mask disguises you, and concealing your face is no longer out of the ordinary. Crime is absolutely connected to all of this.

It's no coincidence that states with the strictest mask policies now have the worst crime!

My question to Cuomo and De Blasio is: How are you going to flatten the curve on all these other things?

How are you going to flatten the curve on deaths of despair?

How are you going to flatten the curve on drug and alcohol abuse?

> Disruptors look at situations differently. When you operate by disrupting, you see the factors at play that others will often choose to ignore.

How are you going to flatten the curve on domestic violence?

And how are you going to flatten the curve on street crime?

There is, you see, more than one curve that needs flattening!

All of these things are plaguing our society today. If I had been in charge, I would not have locked things down. I would not have compelled people to wear masks in situations where it would be advantageous for criminals.

But no, Cuomo and De Blasio went the other way, and now they have no answer for how they are going to flatten the curve on *all these other things* that are killing people!

One of the times I was on Fox Business, I let loose with the "Comrade Cuomo" quip I'd used before. Soon thereafter, one of my business partners got a text from a friend who worked in personal protection near Cuomo.

"Whatever your partner said on Fox, he's really pissed off Cuomo."

I was surprised my words had had such an impact.

Kathy Hochul, then the lt. governor, was also really upset, the same source added. They closed by saying we should be prepared to be raided the following morning.

I knew what that meant.

The next morning, every state agency was in Brooklyn Chop House. It was the Department of Health, the Department of Transportation, the Department of Labor, the Department of Buildings, and the State Liquor Agency—all looking for the slightest infraction they could use to cite me (and, in so doing, please their mafia don, Cuomo). And guess what. They found nothing! I'd already gotten the heads-up, and everything was straight as an arrow.

This just shows you how Cuomo thinks. He retaliates worse than a mobster. He's so sensitive and can't take criticism even when it's only in the form of a nickname. How is this guy a supposed leader?

The only reason I didn't sue him over the raid is that I didn't want to put the person working his personal protection in harm's way, vis-à-vis their career.

* * *

From the moment the mandates hit, I'd been adamant in my position that they don't work.

Now they're telling us that a vax card holder can walk into any establishment safely. The vax card holder is the superspreader. I've gotten so much pushback on this. I was on Fox News with Steve Forbes, and he asked why they were coming out with the Abbott BinaxNOW™ COVID home test now. It had been out for two years. Why? Because of business and money. It was a $10 test, and they wanted to keep it under wraps so they could charge $100. Steve Forbes had the balls to call out that this test had been ready to go, and to ask why it wasn't already on every CVS and Rite Aid shelf.

I went on Tucker Carlson and challenged the governor.

"Arrest me!" I said. "Because I'll never fire someone over this. A jab for a job? It'll never happen!"

I explained that these are the workers who worked for me in 2020 instead of collecting unemployment. They worked for me and fed thousands and thousands of healthcare workers. And now you want to fire them if they didn't get a booster? It's not one-size-fits-all with medicine, just as it isn't with anything else.

I have an employee named Alex who has been with me for fifteen years.

He got the first vaccine, then got COVID and took two weeks to recover. Now he's back at work. He was one of the guys who helped out with shipping hundreds of things for the healthcare heroes. You want me to fire him for not yet having a booster, when *his own doctor* just told him right now that he has an abundance of antibodies because he just had COVID. When my own mother died from a reaction caused by too many antibodies. What about instead letting him postpone the shot for six months, and then letting him take the vaccine.

> Never hesitate to stand up when a rule or law is unjust. You're not the only one who thinks so, but it takes a disruptor to say it out loud.

I was pretty clear on Tucker Carlson that I was defying the mandates and asking to be arrested. I was refusing to fire my staff.

Literally the next day, the Supreme Court came back with a ruling that the mandates were unconstitutional.

I was ahead of the curve! I felt like there was breeze under my wings, and I continued to go on different television shows telling my story about the mandates. It got me a lot of fans. There was a big boost in people buying Brooklyn Chop House merchandise online—I think just because people saw me on TV.

I was defying the rules. Disrupting them. And I sure as hell wasn't firing my staff members *whose own doctors* told them they didn't yet need a second vaccine.

* * *

In conclusion, I hope for a future government in my city that will be brighter for disruptors, as well as for everyone else.

Mayor Eric Adams has said he's going to be probusiness. We'll see.

I recently asked him, "Why should I trust you? I'm a small business owner, and you're a politician. Think about what politicians have done to us over the last two years."

And he gave me what I thought was a great answer.

He said, "I'm a cop, I'm a businessman, and I'm a landlord. And these are the things I'm going to protect and support with all the powers afforded to me by my office. On that, I give you my word."

TAKEAWAYS FOR FUTURE DISRUPTORS

- **Don't wait for someone to tell you what to do in a crisis; get out there and do what you know in your heart is right.**
- **The government is not your friend, and it is *not* here to help you!**

CHAPTER SIXTEEN:

How Disruptors Can Make the Future a Fantastic Place

Let me introduce this final chapter by telling you the last secret to disruption as I understand it. The secret is that all good things— all good success for yourself, all good inventions that change an industry, and so on—come from the urge to help people. When you refine a product, you are helping people. When you take a service that is inefficient and position it in a different way so that it's amazing, you are helping people. When you build a better mousetrap that catches more mice, you are helping people. I'm going to close this book with anecdotes about helping people. I'm going to talk about the need to understand every facet of your business—that's important if you want to help other people, and it's also important if you want to help yourself! And I'm going to talk about the work I am doing to elevate the next generation of disruptors. If we can help others, if we know our businesses, and if we help the next generation, there's nothing that's going to stop us. And we are going to make the world a completely fantastic place!

I wrote this book because I want to help people become better disruptors. I want to lay out the episodes in my own life that have been the most helpful and identify what the lessons are that I took from them. I want to do all this because I genuinely think that what the world needs right now are new paradigms and new ways of thinking. In short, the world needs the things that disruptors bring into being.

This urge to help comes from my father.

I think of the things my father would do to help out struggling restaurants, even ones we were in competition with.

> **Always help others, and always act out of love.**

I'll never forget the first time he took me along on one of these trips. The first thing he did was take their kitchen trash can and turn it upside down. All this stuff went flying everywhere. My father picked through the trash and said: "This is why you're failing. Look at the waste in here." My father found food that could have been repurposed. He found silverware that had been tossed absentmindedly. I remember watching as my father held a swordfish head and showed how meat that had been left on the head could have been pulled off and used to make shish kebobs. (What one man sees as garbage, another sees as revenue!)

For me, this has been the feeling behind this book. I want to share the power of being a disruptor with everyone—even with people who might be my competitors.

* * *

Another of the most important lessons is one I've saved for this last chapter: *Always know every part of your business.*

One day back when I was working in the family restaurant—I was eight years old at the time, still mopping floors—I asked my father, "Why do I have to mop the floors in here? I hate mopping the floors. The note on the menu says: 'Under Morfogen family management.' I'm a member of the Morfogen family. So why do I have to do the worst jobs? Mopping floors. Peeling shrimp. Cleaning the toilets."

And my father said, "If you want to be in this business, you're going to have to do these things. Do you know why? Because you're going to be a manager one day, and you'll have to

> **Knowing every part of your business will ensure that you're able to handle any crisis personally.**

see that other people are doing them correctly. How will you know if they've been done correctly? The answer is that you will do them yourself. You can't learn these things in a book. You can't learn them by watching someone do it once. You have to do all of this yourself."

So I understood at eight years old that I had to do these things myself.

Years later, when I was twelve or thirteen, I got another lesson along those lines. I came into the restaurant on New Year's Eve and heard my father screaming at the kitchen staff. This was at about 4:00 p.m.

It turned out that my father had just given all these guys their usual, end-of-the-year bonuses, but they said they wanted more. If he didn't pay them $1,000 each, they were going to walk out on New Year's Eve, which was probably our biggest day of the year.

So I watched my father send a message, not just to this kitchen staff, but to every other restaurant he had at the time. (He knew word would get around.) My father shouted, "Get the fuck out!" and pointed to the door. He fired all of them. I remember that some left immediately, but others lingered and said they had been led along by the others on this. Could they please still have their jobs? My father said no. If you went against him like that even once, even just tagging along with ringleaders, you were still gone.

My father got on the phone and started calling nephews, cousins, anyone who could come in and work. That night my father took over as head chef, and four or five family members came in and joined him to help us make it through the night under his direction.

Again, the lesson: You need to know the job of every position in your business, or you will find yourself vulnerable.

* * *

I've recently started teaching business courses at universities, and it is now some of the most rewarding work that I do. I've found I really enjoy teaching seventeen-to-twenty-one-year-olds the basics of business. I never went to a university because they didn't teach business, at least not as I knew it. We're one of the only societies that easily allows a student to go into $150,000 worth of debt but makes it hard for a person that age to get $25,000 to do a start-up. What's up with that?

My own daughter is graduating from the University of Miami this year, and I told her, "You're not going to do postgraduate studies. That will be a bad use of your time. Instead, pick the industry of your dreams and work for two years as an intern. You'll learn ten times more in two years of interning than you would getting a master's degree. And you won't go into more debt."

When we had this conversation, my daughter surprised me and said, "Dad, I've actually decided what I want to do."

I said, "Natalie, what is it?"

"I want to work with you," she said. "You inspired me during COVID, and I want to come work with you."

I never expected that. She'd gone to school for marketing and could have gone into any field. I thought she was going to work in real estate.

I had tears running down my face.

"I can't wait," I said.

Her graduation present will be a full equity partnership in Pappas. This way, I know the Pappas name will never leave the Morfogen family again.

* * *

I think my best story to come out of teaching so far happened with a Zoom class at Lehigh University. There was a student named Linda who said, "You're such an inspiration to me, but I'm still so scared to be graduating in this climate."

"Don't be," I told her. "These are the greatest times because opportunities are amazing. If you want to open a restaurant or a retail store, and you can put a decent business plan together, there's a landlord who wants to talk to you. Every landlord has an empty space right now. Things are so dire, the landlord's probably going to put the money up to convert their space into your restaurant, or bar, or flower shop."

"Well, there's also something else I want to ask about, but it's more personal to me," Linda said.

"What is it?" I asked.

"It's my dad," she said. "He's sixty-two, and he had an Italian restaurant for thirty-five years on the Upper East Side. He just lost it. During COVID, he had to shut down, and the landlord took possession. Now I can't get him off the couch. He's in full depression. He feels that at sixty-two he can't just

> **When you know what it's like to need a kick in the ass, you won't hesitate to administer one when it's called for!**

go get a regular job; he's been an entrepreneur for thirty-five years. I'm worried about him. What advice do I give him? I feel like he could do something stupid because he's really depressed."

"Linda," I said, "get on your sharpest boots, and polish and shine the tips of them, go up to that couch, and kick your father in the ass as hard as you can. Kick him until he jumps up and screams. Then, when he's up, I want you to tell him that I've got twenty-five landlords who want to speak to him."

"What do you mean?" she said.

"You said he owned an Italian restaurant for thirty-five years," I said.

"Yes," she said.

"Well, let me tell you something about being an entrepreneur," I told her. "Politicians and their policies can trample on the rights of working people. They couldn't care less whether or not their policies ruin people. They couldn't care less if entrepreneurs can put food on the table. But one thing they can't take away from your father is his intellectual property. They can't take away the fact that he ran a successful restaurant on the Upper East Side for thirty-five years. Not everybody has a thirty-five-year run. And the only reason he lost it— which he should not be ashamed of—is that these dirtbag politicians, who never ran anything, swooped in and shut everyone down. You tell your father that I can introduce him to twenty-five landlords who will not just have a meeting with him, but who'll put the red carpet out and treat him like royalty because he ran a successful business for thirty-five years. I'm telling you, your dad has a lot of value left. There's a lot of gas in that tank. People say that sixty-two is old or is an age for retirement, but they wrote those rules in 1901, that you should make your money in your twenties and retire in your sixties. Bullshit! You should lose everything you've got in your twenties, learn from it, grow your brand in your thirties and forties, and work 'til you're ninety if you want to. Because those rules were created when the average lifespan was sixty-seven. Today it's eighty-four. So those rules don't apply anymore. So, tell your dad that if he wants the introduction, I'll make the introduction."

After class, I sent Linda to five or six landlords. And then, honestly, I forgot about it. I had other things on my plate. But then six months later, I got an invite. It turns out Linda's dad is opening a restaurant seven blocks away from his original restaurant. And Linda informs me that the landlord paid for everything.

Who knows what would have happened to Linda's father? Because I've been there. I've been the guy on the couch thinking it was all over. Feeling like I didn't want to wake up anymore. I understand that. We entrepreneurs are so passionate about our businesses, and then when someone—whether a politician or a corrupt partner—rips them away, you just feel gutted. It's easy to feel like there was no value to all the years you worked. But there *is* value. Your accomplishments can never be stolen.

* * *

I want helping other entrepreneurs to be part of my legacy, because I know what it is to need some help. And I know how powerful receiving that help can be. People need to be inspired, and they need to hear about inspiration. That will be a part of whatever I do for the rest of my life.

In the shorter term, helping others has brought my life to new heights. In 2022, I've been asked to speak at over twenty hospitality industry conferences. I've been named a Top 100 trendsetter in hospitality tech; a top entrepreneur to look out for in 2022; and I'm even in negotiations to star in my own television show about disruption in business.

I can't resist closing with a funny story about that . . . When Universal came to me with their first offer for the terms of the show, it was a terrible deal. My lawyer and I went back to the production company and said, "We have to reject this offer because the terms are so bad. Anyone who does agree to terms like these shouldn't be on a show about being good at business!" Ha!

TAKEAWAYS FOR FUTURE DISRUPTORS

- **Success comes from helping other people.**
- **Know every part of your business; there are a million reasons why you should, and no good reasons not to.**
- **Extend a hand down the ladder and help the next generation of disruptors.**

Stratis's Rules for Disruptors

- Never let success go to your head and never let failure take over your heart.
- If you want to be an entrepreneur, you have to have thick skin.
- If your dreams do not scare the fuck out of you, then they aren't big enough.
- You have to decide what 5:00 a.m. means to you. Are you coming home from a night of partying, or are you getting up to start a new day with your hustle on? That can be the difference between success and failure.
- If the door doesn't open the first few times you knock on it, kick it the fuck down!
- The 97 percent of people who quit are now working for the 3 percent who refused to quit.

- Think outside the box in an industry you love. Create a better mousetrap. Embrace technology, like we did at Brooklyn Dumpling Shop and Brooklyn Chop House.
- Embrace tech, especially in industries that have traditionally be late to embrace tech advancements.
- Jump into the fire! Don't run from it.
- Set goals and hit your mark. If you give yourself three days to read a book, read it in three days. If you give yourself eighteen months to open a restaurant, open it in eighteen months (even if you have to live inside its construction site, something I've done many times)!
- You will never succeed with a forty-hour workweek. You will remain a sheep. As my dad used to say, "Half days are twelve-hour days." Luck happens when opportunity meets preparation, and luck happens when you work hard and long. My take is that working sixty hours a week makes you pretty lucky.
- If you want to be liked and live comfortably, you will never be an entrepreneur and you will never be a boss.
- Don't listen to the outside noise. Stay focused on your goals. I was ranked 343 out of 345 in my high school class, but I knew what I wanted to do and I knew how to do it.
- Shame on universities when they teach you how to be a nameless VP operating and stuck somewhere inside the status quo, as opposed to how to be an entrepreneur. Corporate VPs only get to live somebody else's dream.
- If you want to be a successful entrepreneur, make moves to educate yourself. Be proactive. Don't wait for others to teach you. Remember that most of the people teaching business classes have never run their own businesses. Take control of your growth by reading.

- Money can buy you a clock, but not time. I'm learning to manage my time; 4,400 weeks goes pretty fast if you want to live to eighty-five.
- It doesn't matter whether you win or lose . . . as long as you win.
- The two key ingredients to success are timing and execution.
- Stay humble. Stay hungry. And remember that it's okay to be alone.
- Don't ever look back; it fucks with your neck!
- It's actually good manners to cut someone short when you have no interest in having a conversation with them. You're not wasting each other's time. I strongly believe in cutting people off quickly.
- The first one through the wall gets the bloody nose. Always expect to be the first one through the wall!
- Never give up, ever. I've been in depression. I've been inside the abyss. I hit rock bottom in 2013 and 2014. *And I came back!* Always remember, right when you're just about to give up is when the miracle happens. I'm living proof.

My grandfather didn't have a pair of shoes until he was twelve years old.

My father played soccer barefoot with a big stone for a soccer ball in the mountains of war-torn, Nazi-occupied Sparta before getting his first pair of shoes when he was ten years old.

I drive a Porsche.

My daughter drives a Mercedes.

And my grandchild will drive a Ferrari.

My great-grandchild will be shoeless again.

"Why?" is the question I'm asked. Why would I say such a thing?

My answer: Tough times create strong men. Strong men create easy times. Easy times create weak men. Weak men create tough times.

Most will not understand this, but this lesson goes to the future Morfogen generations reading this book to raise our kids into warriors.